Forgiveness is a gift that you give to yourself.

Hope and inspiration is a gift that you give to others.

Beyond CHERRY MOUNTAIN

FAMILY, FAITH, AND FORGIVENESS

Lily Brassica

WESTBOW PRESS®
A DIVISION OF THOMAS NELSON & ZONDERVAN

WestBow Press books may be ordered through booksellers or by contacting:

WestBow Press
A Division of Thomas Nelson & Zondervan
1663 Liberty Drive
Bloomington, IN 47403
www.westbowpress.com
1 (866) 928-1240

ISBN: 978-1-9736-3399-0 (sc)
ISBN: 978-1-9736-3401-0 (hc)
ISBN: 978-1-9736-3400-3 (e)

Library of Congress Control Number: 2018908243

Print information available on the last page.

WestBow Press rev. date: 08/28/2018

Contents

Preface

Beyond Cherry Mountain tells the true story of a woman who was born into humble surroundings in a small community in North Carolina. The story starts after she learns about Jesus and the surroundings in which he was born. She feels he is a kindred spirit, and she embarks on a quest to learn more about him. As she does, she yearns to be adopted by his heavenly Father and vows to serve God for eternity.

Dressed in clothes made from feed sacks, wearing shoes held together with duct tape and cardboard, and having little to eat, she considers God as the one thing she can count on for her protection and basic needs.

In her story, the mountains are a metaphor for success and the valleys are a metaphor for the trials we all go through. She sometimes finds herself climbing these mountains with faith no bigger than a mustard seed as she faces loose boulders and landslides as she ascends the mountains. She often ends up in the valley, where Jesus is her only friend.

Born with a stubborn determination and armed with only the love for Jesus in her heart, she commits her life to God and vows to do something meaningful that will open others' eyes to the awesome God she serves.

Some of the mountains she climbs are personal and family illnesses. One mountain in particular is a goal to become a cosmetologist. When God first spoke to her heart and instructed her to become a cosmetologist, she questioned him, but after becoming a confident hairdresser, she realizes her workstation made a great pulpit to share Jesus and all the wonderful blessings she receives because of her faith.

She shares her stories with everyone who sits in her chair. She has spent her life being obedient, and when God spoke to her heart and told her to write a book full of forgiveness, inspiration, faith, hope, sacrifice, and reward, she began taking notes.

This is her story.

1
Cherry Mountain Childhood

All over the world, melting glaciers reveal scars in the earth. Over time, the scars disappear as vegetation reshapes the landscape with a new look—a rebirth. That's how I think of the Great Depression and the scars it left.

In the 1950s, healing was underway in the south, and as were the scars left by the glaciers, new hope and opportunities were emerging. In North Carolina, the deepest scars were still visible; families were struggling to acquire their versions of the American Dream. Some wanted to live in cities or suburbs while others wanted to live in the country with enough land to raise a family.

Their versions of the American Dream were limited only by the imaginations. The opportunity to acquire it seemed achievable with hard work and determination, but doing that in light of their limited education and their circumstances they suffered during the Depression was a lifetime commitment.

My parents were among them; both had been born to poor families. Dad was one of twelve children; he started working at a sawmill at age nine to help his family survive, and that left him with only a third-grade education. Mom was one of seven; living closer to town, she was fortunate enough to end up with a tenth-grade education.

My parents met when my mom was sixteen and my dad was twenty-two. After a short courtship, they married and started a family. My parents' first child was a girl. In the eighth month of that pregnancy, my mom caught the German measles; the infant was born very weak and unfortunately died when she was three months old.

My parents' version of the American Dream was to own a parcel of land outside town with enough room for a large garden and farm animals. In the late 1950s, they realized that dream with the purchase of a thirty-acre parcel twenty miles from the nearest town.

By that time, my parents had four very energetic boys all blessed with bubbly personalities they had inherited from their father. The land my parents purchased had an old shack strategically placed in the corner along with a few old barns. The creek at the far end of the property initially served as our only source of water.

The four-room shack was less than a thousand square feet and consisted of two bedrooms, a kitchen, and a living room. Because they had no indoor plumbing, during the winter, the toilet was a honey bucket in the corner of a bedroom. In the warmer months, the great outdoors—well, I'll leave that up to your imagination. My father eventually dug a well by hand that was closer to the shack than was the creek. The well had a simple structure built over the top to allow a bucket on a rope to be lowered into the well; that made it possible for even a child to draw water.

Ceramic lightbulb holders hung from the ceiling in each room; the wire, which looped over some bent nails, ran through the wall to the service outside. An old cookstove that burned wood sat in the kitchen, which had no cabinets—just some shelves.

My dad built our kitchen table from scrap lumber; chairs were simply blocks of indestructible firewood lined up around the table. The shack's broken windows had nothing covering them, and the gaps in the walls and flooring were wide enough to feed chickens through, but in my parents' minds, they had achieved their version of the American Dream. The shack kept them warm and dry, and that was enough.

In the early 1960s, I was born into these humble surroundings. My crib was a dresser drawer lined with a quilt my mama had made from scraps of cloth. Dad and Mom always believed that I was a little miracle sent by God to fill the void left behind by the death of their firstborn. Under the protection of my four older brothers, I developed a strong, courageous personality based on faith and tenacity.

Two economic blessings contributed to the growth of North Carolina—furniture factories and textile mills. The wood and cotton these industries relied on were harvested throughout the south and created an economic boom that generated opportunities for employment—a true gift from God.

Workers were needed for a variety of other jobs including some with the state and the power company. North Carolina was in dire need of new infrastructure including new power grids to keep up with the increasing demand for electricity. My dad played an important role in the expansion of the power grid across North Carolina. His job was to help build huge metal towers and pull the wire from tower to tower by using his two horses, Blondie and Jube.

My dad and the horses would be gone pulling wire across the state for weeks at a time. Life was hard growing up with my dad being gone so much. We didn't have any of the conveniences that would have made things easier, but our tight-knit group of siblings didn't know any differently, so we all simply pitched in and handled our daily chores—drawing water from the well, chopping firewood for cooking and heat, and feeding the livestock—cows for milk, hogs for our winter meat, chickens for eggs and an occasional Sunday dinner, and rabbits that multiplied quickly to keep us supplied with protein.

Where we lived may have looked like a shack, but it was our home, and it was blessed by what we had—a lot of love for each other.

The stove didn't have any fancy buttons to control the temperature, but my mother made some of the best vittles by using old-school recipes with variously a smidgen, a pinch, a little bit, a middling amount, a right smart, and a whole heap of ingredients that would turn out the most beautiful bread and delicious meals I have ever eaten.

I don't remember the blocks of firewood that lined the table as being all that comfortable, but we didn't sit at the table to relax—we sat to eat what had been prepared. A water bucket and dipper sat on a little table in the kitchen on which was as well a metal wash pan we used as a sink and as a washbasin. Ours wasn't an environment anyone who was afraid of germs could live in.

We never went to the doctor's unless we were suffering from something really serious. My dad treated us with the same medicine he used on our animals. If home remedies that had been passed down from generations living off the land didn't work, he would try liniment or possibly castor oil he bought from a traveling salesman. If we were still sick after all that, we were in trouble. If one of us young 'uns got a cough, that called for a teaspoon of moonshine and rock candy. My dad would say, "If it doesn't cure you, it'll kill you, but you'll be okay either way." God must have blessed us with strong immune systems because we were hardly ever sick.

In addition to doing all our chores, we also had to stay clean—that was an imperative. It was much easier in the summer than in the winter because we used the creek for bathing and washing our clothes. But in the winter, bathing and laundering were quite the chores. We did have an old wringer washer on the back porch, but with no running water, we all had to draw enough water to fill the washer and the multipurpose bathing and rinsing tub we stored behind the stove.

We would heat the water we used for bathing, but we washed clothes in cold water. Our clothesline seemed to stretch on forever next to the house. We assembled a work brigade to send the clothes through the wringer to get the excess water out and hang them on the clothesline to dry outside.

Our cookstove wasn't our only source of heat; an old, wood-burning heater we named Haskell sat in the living room, and it blessed the rest of the house with its warmth. An insurance salesman came by one day to try to sell my parents homeowners' insurance. When the salesman asked about insulation, my dad replied, "All we have is what the birds and squirrels have brought in over the years."

We five kids and our parents were living in close quarters. We slept under quilts that we had all pitched in and made by using a quilting frame that hung by ropes from the living room ceiling; we'd lower it when we wanted to work on a quilt. The quilts kept us warm and cozy throughout the cold winters. Occasionally when it snowed, the wind would blow the snow through the cracks and we'd wake up covered with snow. We slept fully dressed so we wouldn't freeze to death when we got up in the morning.

Our family didn't always own a tractor, so in the spring when the daffodils started to bloom, we knew it was time to prepare the land for our crops. Daddy would plow rows with the help of our horses; we depended on our thirty acres to provide food for our animals as well as ourselves. We planted several acres of corn primarily for animal feed, but dried corn was sent to the hammermill where it was made into cornmeal for making cornbread.

Our vegetable garden was so big that we children could get lost in it. My dad purchased fertilizer from a farm center to nourish the rows of green beans, tomatoes, radishes, turnips, potatoes, cabbage, and just about anything else we could find seeds for. We couldn't use the creek for irrigating the garden, so spring rains and occasional rainstorms determined how well we ate any one winter. It took the cooperation and diligence of the entire family to weed the garden and prepare the vegetables for canning, which my mom handled—hundreds of jars to last us through the winter.

We children weren't that old before we realize where most of our food was coming from, so we learned early on to keep an eye out for animals that would regularly attempt to raid our garden. You might say I was the family llama when it came to being an early warning system when it came to intruders. Some of those intruders ended up in a large pot along with the vegetables they were trying to steal because eventually, just as was the case with my siblings, I became a pretty good shot with a .22 rifle. I was proud of all the hard work we were doing to make that shack and property our home, and I didn't let anything destroy it.

My dad didn't waste any of our acreage growing hay for our animals; instead, he traded his labor with dairy farmers in exchange for enough hay to get our animals through the winter. As the boys got old and strong enough, they would buck those bales of hay—hundreds of them—and would assist my dad whenever he worked in the fields. As soon as I was big enough, I did that as well.

A big, yellow school bus showed up each day when I started first grade to take me from the farm to a world of knowledge and endless possibilities. I was introduced to a life beyond what I had grown to know as normal, and I began to dream of someday leaving the farm to make my own way in the world.

2
Forever in My Heart

I learned all about Thanksgiving in first grade. Until then, that holiday merely meant I had to say goodbye to a friend I had been feeding the past year—Thanksgiving was hog-killing time for us.

When I'd wake up on Thanksgiving morning, my dad would already have a hog slaughtered and a fire built under a fifty-five-gallon drum of water used for loosening the hair to make it easier to scrape off.

Our wooden singletree hung from a limb of the big oak tree in our front yard. A singletree is a wood or metal bar used in a horses' harness to which the ends of the reins were attached for plowing. My dad used it also to hang slaughtered hogs upside down by their hooves so he could butcher them.

I always knew when hog-butchering day was approaching because the weather would be getting cooler and most of the leaves would have fallen. I had a love-hate feeling for that day. I hated to say goodbye to one of the hogs, but it was also a beginning for a young pig I would feed in the barn in preparation for the next year.

Everyone in our family was up to his or her elbows in work the entire day, but if as a family we prepared the meat correctly, we'd have meat all winter. The hog had to be slaughtered, butchered, salt-cured, and hung in the smokehouse to preserve the meat because we never had a freezer.

We also got cooking lard for the year by cooking the hog's fat. Mom would put various "extra" pieces of the hog into a pot to cook for when we were finished. "Extra" meant the heart, kidney, lungs, and ears. Those parts of the hog along with vegetables we had canned were our version of the traditional Thanksgiving dinner of turkey with all the fixings. In a sense, we were celebrating the traditional Thanksgiving holiday that went back to the Pilgrims at Plymouth that was prompted by their good harvest.

I went to school each day wearing clothing made from hog feed sacks my mother fashioned using needle, thread, and her creative talents. I thought that was how everyone lived until I learned differently from the other children at school.

Mama had an old treadle sewing machine that was powered by a pedal she would operate with her feet. She would stay up late every night at the end of summer sewing clothes for the new school year. We all got two pairs of store-bought britches—pants—and my mom would make us two shirts each out of feed sacks. We also got one pair of $2.50 shoes per year. We never got to go along when my parents went clothes shopping. My dad simply used a length of string to measure our waists and legs for pants and a hickory stick to measure our feet for shoes.

My mom's fingers would get sore, and she would occasionally leave a drop or two of blood in the seams of our clothing. The color and design on the feed sack determined whether the sack would become boy or girl clothes. The sacks' fabric was normally white or cream colored. The prints on the sacks would be pastels or darker colors more appropriate for boys. My mom would always make me a dress, which meant I'd get only one pair of pants, but I loved dresses; I was glad to give up a pair of britches for a dress.

We didn't have a closet in our house, so by the time school

started, the broomstick in the corner of our bedroom would sag under the weight of all our new clothes hanging on it. We were so proud of our new clothes and were appreciative of all Mom's hard work.

We took good care of our clothes especially our shoes because we wouldn't get new ones until the next year. When they began to show wear and tear, we'd stuff the insides with cardboard and bind them with duct tape. But no matter how hard we tried to take care of our clothes, they'd be totally worn out by the end of the school year. Thank God for summer—the boys didn't wear shirts then, and my clothes were whatever was still hanging together. We all went barefoot. We never got to enjoy many hand-me-downs.

I loved school—I learned new things and met new people. I don't believe we cross paths with people by chance; I believe God strategically places people in our paths for specific reasons. I can look back over the years and tell you every person God carefully put in my path, people who helped mold me into the person I am today. I am a giver because of the people God used to meet my needs.

My first experience with God helping me through others was when I needed a winter coat for school; I'd freeze while waiting for the school bus each morning. The driveway was much too long for me to wait in the house, so God laid it on the school librarian's heart to take me to get a coat. I learned that God helps those who aren't able to help themselves through the kindness of others. When God's people are obedient, we receive the biggest blessings.

I am a compassionate and understanding person who has a relationship with God today because of my petite first-grade teacher, my first example of what a Christian should be. She began each day by reading us stories of love, hope, and encouragement from her big, heavy Bible. She read stories of a

Savior by the name of Jesus, whom God sent as his Son to earth; he gave his life so we could be saved.

We always said a blessing before going to lunch; that taught us how to pray at a young age. She read to us about heaven and about Jesus going back to his home to prepare a place for his children. She would challenge us to memorize Bible verses that had significant meaning for us, for instance, verses that started with the first letters of our names. If your name started with an *B*, you would memorize a verse that started with that letter.

She read about a wonderful holiday called Easter, which celebrated Jesus's resurrection from the dead. Easter always reminds me of spring and new beginnings. In the south, spring comes with warmer weather and showers. Easter comes at the time of year when our land needed to be plowed for the new growing season. We always put our seeds in the ground on Good Friday. All the trees would be budding with new life. Everywhere we looked, color was emerging and transforming the landscape into a vibrant reminder of Jesus's resurrection.

The first sign Easter was approaching was the daffodils that would start poking up through the ground. We never had a lawn, but our patches of grass mixed with bunches of beautiful yellow flowers were always a welcome sight.

The Easter Bunny never brought baskets of colored eggs and candy to our house, but knowing the meaning of Easter was a true gift. I was celebrating the cross of Jesus Christ. By his crucifixion, Jesus paid the ultimate price for our sins. Every lashing he took with that cat o' nine tails was meant to heal us physically and spiritually. He gave his life unselfishly so we might live, and his resurrection meant he was no longer in the tomb, hallelujah!

I think the most beautiful part of the Easter story was that the cross Jesus carried became a bridge between heaven and earth so that when our lives were over here on earth, we could live eternally in heaven with him. That Jesus was sacrificed for the sins of the world according to his Father's plan shows me there is no greater love.

She read us the promise in the Bible that all we had to do to receive these beautiful blessings was to believe. She taught us the value of asking Jesus to forgive our sins and come into our hearts to live forever. It sounded simple to me; my heart was the one thing I had to offer.

Every day, she would pull that big book off the shelf and teach us something about God and Jesus. I fell in love with Jesus and wanted to learn as much as I could about him because that gave me hope and inspiration. I wasn't the only one to benefit from the teachings; all the other children in class did so as well. She taught us it didn't matter to Jesus whether we were privileged or underprivileged—he loved us all the same. Learning about Jesus changed my life.

I know in my heart that my dad would have loved to read me the Bible, but he couldn't read or write. But he had had a good Christian family upbringing and a strong belief in God, and he also had good moral values he lived by. I believe if he would've had the ability, he might have played a larger role in helping me study God's Word.

He was a loving, kind, and generous man; no one left our home after visiting without something in his or her hand no matter how little he had to share. It would often be as simple as vegetables from the garden or some fresh pork from a pig he had just butchered. He was a six-foot-two gentle giant and my hero. He always smiled no matter the situation. He taught me the important things in life such as respecting and treating others as you would like to be treated. He taught us manners and to always say please and thank you. I learned to work hard and never compromise my ethics or morals just by watching my dad back then. I was always eager to listen to his teachings. When I was young, he would sit me on his lap and wrap me in his old coat that he referred to as his dog bed, and we would talk for hours.

My dad was always a great example of who I wanted to be. He was a patient and understanding man, but like the rest of us, he had hurdles to overcome, the hardest of which was a wife who was slowly giving up on the dreams and goals they had set for themselves.

3 The Transformation

Until the late sixties, my mom stayed at home raising her family. Though my mom's parents had been alcoholics who preferred moonshine to food, she had somehow acquired loving, nurturing parenting skills that had transformed our little four-room shack into a home full of love and joy. We were a happy family; we had each other though we lived a simple life.

I can imagine how lonely and hard life must have been for Mom when Dad was away for weeks at a time. She had no outlet. If we were lucky, we were able to watch a black-and-white TV by means of a drop cord and a rabbit-ears antenna with some aluminum foil wrapped around it to improve reception. Some of my fondest memories of my mom were when we would let down the quilting frame from the living room ceiling and work on a quilt on Saturday nights while watching *Hee-Haw*.

My mom's loving, nurturing side started to unravel when a friend of hers started coming over to our house on a fairly regular basis. She introduced my mom to a different side of life. My mom's friend was a bit on the rough side to put it mildly. I won't go into every bad decision she ever made, but once, she attacked a man in some establishment where alcohol was sold, and she went to prison. She wasn't a good influence on my mom to say the least.

Our county was dry—no alcohol could be bought or sold in it, but bootleggers would distill moonshine from corn and sell it in glass pint or quart jars or in gallon plastic jugs. They also made moonshine from fresh cherries grown locally and called it cherry bounce. They'd open makeshift nightclubs called nip joints in their houses. They'd remove the furniture from at least one room, move in a jukebox, and have a makeshift bar lined with stools. Such nip joints were scattered all over our county and were responsible for keeping the beer and moonshine flowing but took no responsibility for the lives their alcohol was leaving in shambles.

I believe my mom was at a vulnerable stage in her life at that time, and the loneliness along with her responsibilities of keeping her family warm, dry, fed, and clothed were overwhelming. I don't think it was hard for her friend to convince my mom that the answer to her problems was at the bottom of a glass jar.

From the moment my mom took that first drink, our lives as we knew them changed forever. I pray regularly for God to protect the children of this world from ever having to witness those they love changing in front of their eyes with each swallow of alcohol. As a child, I was frightened to see the transformation that took place with every drink she had.

Alcohol robbed my mom of her ability to think logically, and as a result, her parenting skills disappeared. Her priorities begin to shift from making sure she prepared meals for her children to whether her belly was full of the liquid corn that sat on the table where our food used to sit.

It didn't take my dad long to figure out what was going on—his children were being neglected by the woman he once held in high regard. He would drive home from wherever he was working regardless of the distance to make sure we had something to eat. He got very little rest, and his feet would swell so much that he couldn't take his boots off.

We ate a lot of fried potatoes. My dad always planted sweet

potatoes so we kids could enjoy something hot and sweet. I still consider sweet potatoes a dessert; I fondly remember my dad whenever I eat one. No matter what my dad prepared for us, it always took away our hunger pangs and filled up that hollow spot in our tummies.

In the summer, we would scrounge for food around the neighborhood. Driven by hunger, we ate every wild plum and picked every berry bush until it was bare. My brothers would hunt squirrels and rabbits to help keep us fed. Every morning, we were out hunting for the eggs our free-range chickens would lay overnight. We grazed on the fruit from the few apple trees near our house, and we'd do so before it had ripened.

It's sad to think that one of my most joyous discoveries as a child was that mixing flour and water would make a hoe cake. It was only bread, but it was very filling. My uncle would come to visit, and more often than not, he would have some type of little sweet cakes for us to enjoy.

Alcohol robbed my mom of her desire to nurture us kids; it also robbed us of the lives we once knew. The new reality we kids lived was confusing. Our mom would transform from a saint to a devil with every sip of alcohol right in front of our eyes. We never knew what we were coming home to after school. She would go from loving us one moment to wanting to kill us the next, and that was very hard for us children to understand. God tells us to honor our parents, but that is hard to do with parents who are not deserving of honor because of their actions.

One time in the late sixties, I become very ill and was running a high fever. My dad was working out of town at the time. My mom tried all the old family remedies but to no avail; she had no choice but to take me to the doctor. I was diagnosed with rheumatic fever, which can develop as a complication of inadequately treated strep throat. If left untreated, it could cause permanent damage to the heart and other organs.

The doctor told my mom that if my fever didn't break by

midnight, I'd have to be hospitalized and put in isolation. I believed I would be okay if my dad came home. When my mom sent him a message about my situation; he immediately told his supervisor he was going home to care for me. His supervisor said that he'd lose his job if he did, but my dad was very family orientated. He didn't explain his urgent reason for going home; he just accepted the circumstances he was facing and rushed home.

My dad knew that my mom was untrustworthy and that one stop at the nip joint could mean the difference between life and death for his little girl. My mom was so addicted to alcohol at that time that she even had a way to get moonshine delivered to her if she had a hankering for some. A local bootlegger would bring her anything she wanted in trade for some canned goods and meat. We children watched in fear as our only supply of food went out the door.

Thank God my dad always put his family first. With medicine from the doctor and a small bottle of cola my dad had in his truck, by midnight, my fever was gone. I feel God used my illness to bring my dad home to stay. Because my mom was no longer trustworthy, my dad didn't think twice about staying home and starting a small logging business with a two-ton truck and tractor with a set of forks for lifting the logs. My dad may not have had an education, but he was a hard worker and could do anything he set his mind to.

4
Jesus in My Heart, Angel at My Side

Once my dad started his business, my mom went to work at a textile mill, but that was not to improve anyone's living conditions but hers. Our lives remained the same; we didn't know from one day to the next if we would have enough to eat or if it was going to be the day our mom actually hit us with one of the bullets or knives she frequently sent our direction.

She would work all week, but as soon as Friday rolled around, she would stop at the beauty shop to get her hair all fixed up for her weekend adventures. She always bought herself fancy purses and nice clothes to wear to the nip joints despite what we kids were wearing. When she pulled into the driveway after driving home from work, we could hear all the country greats blaring from her car. It was obvious that she wasn't trying to keep it a secret that she was preparing for the weekend. She always drove a car with a V-8 engine in case she needed to outrun the law.

At some point when I was very young and for a reason that's still a mystery to me, she began to demand that more often than not I was to go with her on her two-day benders. I can't remember exactly when it started, but I was the one Mom would choose to go with her. She knew I hated going with her, so she would lie to me and say we were just going to the store. Because she was my mom, I wanted to believe her, but it never took her long to abandon me at all sorts of dangerous locations. The weekends were long—from Friday night until Sunday night. Where we ended up was simply according to which direction my mom chose to drive.

All the nip joints had names like Sugar Shack, Joe's Place, and The Hole. They all offered the same services, and they were all off the main road in the trees so as not to be obvious to the neighbors. Sometimes, I wonder if she forced me to go with her on these excursions because she needed someone to light her cigarettes or pop the tops off her beer cans while she was driving down some old country road.

Besides that cough medicine I was given as a child, I have never tasted alcohol or smoked cigarettes, but I shudder to think of how many cigarettes I lit or beer cans I had to pop the top off for her. Only by the grace of God and my friend, Jesus, have I always stayed away from that lifestyle, and I'm thankful for that.

It wasn't unusual for my mom to be driving down some country road drifting around curves, and we didn't always make it around the corner; every now and then, we'd slide into the ditch or bump another car off the road. Her driving skills didn't increase along with her alcohol consumption, but our speed sure seemed to.

I always thought the right thing to do was to wave at other cars as we passed them; that's what my dad did. But riding with my mom was different; she would warn me against what she called throwing up my hand. She would say, "Don't you go throwing up your hand at any police officers," but she would use colorful names for the police. She just didn't want me drawing their attention.

My mom was fearless under the influence of liquid courage. Sometimes at night, she would turn the headlights off to lose the cops. I know God assigned me a guardian angel because I could feel his presence on those long weekend trips.

There was no reasoning with her while she was in that frame of mind. If she couldn't get the car into drive, she would simply put it in reverse and continue on her way. She was determined to get down the road, and it didn't matter to her which end of the car got there first. She once drove thirty miles in reverse. My guardian angel was working overtime to save me on that road trip.

I have even found myself in jail, and going to jail as a child isn't fun. We didn't always have a phone at our home for me to call my dad for help. The closest phone was at my uncle's house, and he lived a distance away. If I wasn't able to reach anyone to come and pick me up, I would just have to hang out at the jail until my mom was released or I was finally able to reach someone.

One time, she was arrested for DUI. Back in the day, it must have been easier to change your identity than it is today because after her DUI, she had me change the color of her hair with a box of hair coloring. I believe that was my first experience with being a hair stylist. After we changed my mom's hair color, she somehow got another driver's license by changing her name, address, and birthdate. She didn't change anything by very much—just a letter here and a number there. By the next week, she was as good as new and back on those ol' country roads looking for her next adventure.

As a child, I found it hard to watch my mom hanging onto different men she would meet at the nip joints especially when I knew she had a wonderful husband back home with the rest of the family.

When my mom and I left home on Friday evenings, the only reassuring thing about the entire weekend was that it always ended in time for her to be back at work on Monday mornings. I'm so grateful I was introduced to my best friend, Jesus, at such a young age. I thank God for being with me and for sending his guardian angel to protect me.

My mom left me in all kinds of places. It wasn't uncommon for me to be in the parked car in the middle of a broom sage field in the middle of nowhere and at the end of a dead-end road for the entire weekend with no food or water. I was once abandoned at the county fair and had to find my own way home. After being in similar situations, I memorized my uncle's phone number.

At other times, my mom would simply leave me at a bootlegger's house twirling on some barstools surrounded by inebriated strangers while she ran off somewhere in the car. When that happened, I would hide in the hedges beside the porch or behind the house out of sight trying to be as quiet as a mouse. I wasn't worried just about strangers that might have hurt me; deadly snakes and insects were common in the south. But my guardian angel was always there to protect me even in the thickest brush and darkest night.

Among my greatest fears when my mom would leave me in one of those precarious locations was that something would happen to her and I would never be found or that because of all her alcohol consumption, she would simply forget where she had left me.

I was always afraid of the dark, so when night would fall and I couldn't see my hand in front of my face, I would pray. I believe that is when I developed my close relationship with God. I would repeat Bible verses I had learned at school, and I would pray, "Dear Jesus, you are my light in these moments of darkness. Please don't leave me. Let me hold your hand." I would pray until God's sweet Spirit filled my soul. I knew God's Spirit was real because I could feel his presence. Only then could I go to sleep.

In all my adventures with my mom, I was never abducted or harmed. At times, I would see drunk men wandering around the area I would be stashed in, and being just a little girl, I felt helpless. I now know that God put a hedge of protection around me because not even once did one of those men see me in the car or in the hedges.

The days were long and boring, so if I was somewhere I didn't have to be quiet, I sang the songs I learned in church and talked to my friend, Jesus, who was as real to me as anything I could see or touch. I never physically saw him, but I felt his presence, and that was enough.

My classmates and I were challenged to learn the Ten Commandments. It seemed like a huge task at first, but the more I studied them, the more I wanted to learn. I spent hours memorizing them and started to incorporate them into my everyday life. The day finally came when I could stand in front of the class and recite them by heart. The teacher rewarded me with the balloon, but she gave me way more than a balloon.

By then, I knew everything about those weekend excursions was wrong, and I took advantage of every opportunity to share what I had learned. Once, I was dropped off in the middle of town on the sidewalk because I didn't like the fact my mom had a boyfriend. As I sat there in the dark not knowing what to do next, I felt helpless, but God knew exactly where I was, and he sent me help.

I saw someone walking up the sidewalk towards me. I now know it was my guardian angel showing up disguised as a police officer. I know that because he didn't ask me any questions. His voice was calm and comforting. It was as if he knew me and my situation. He simply said he would take me home. It's a good thing he didn't ask a lot of questions because I'd been trained not to give police officers any information. But I felt so comfortable around him that I volunteered my dad's name and a vague description of where I lived. But I feel in my heart that he already knew that. That was the last time I ever rode in a police car.

I wanted mom's boyfriend out of our lives so badly that I prayed to God to do that. On one occasion, I took matters into my own hands by raddling my mom's boyfriends cage when she stepped out of the car, grabbed a buggy-shopping cart-and ran into the store for a minute. When my mom returned, she found her boyfriend unconscious and realized he wasn't going to be any fun, so she opened the door and with the assistance of her two legs and feet, let him out. At least that got rid of him for the rest of the weekend. After that, I gave the situation back to God and asked him to forgive me for my lack of faith.

For obvious reasons, it was better to be abandoned in a vehicle than to have to hide in the hedges. In the south, summer days can be very hot, and children have died after being left in cars. I had been left in the car for more than two days at a time more often than I care to remember, but I've never been so hot that it was unbearable. My mom would take the keys to the car with her so I wouldn't wear the battery down trying to figure out how to start the car or run the car out of gas if I managed to get it started. My mom didn't have the presence of mind to care for me, but my heavenly Father knew exactly where I was despite my mom's effort to hide me. No matter where I was, my guardian angel never left my side. At the end of a long night when the sun would come up, I knew I had been blessed with a new day.

Every now and then, I would be left at a particular bootlegger's nip joint that was hosted by a special woman. I'll never forget the kindness she extended to me. Whenever she saw my mom in her nip joint, she came looking for me and made sure I had food, light, and warmth, and for that I will always be grateful.

My mom would lose the ability to think logically when she was nipping on the moonshine. She would tell my dad where she had been and what she had done. I can only assume she did that to antagonize him, or possibly in her own way, she blamed him for the way her life had turned out. No matter what her reasons were, by the next weekend, my dad would be so angry that he would be at the breaking point. He would insist I stay home despite my mother's protests. She knew I had her routine memorized and could lead him to her favorite hangouts. She was right; that was what my dad expected me to do. It didn't take a genius to figure out what he was going to do when and if I led him to where my mom and her boyfriend were hanging out.

When my dad laid his rifle on the dash of the truck and instructed me to start taking him to the nip joints, I prayed really hard we wouldn't find them. On at least one occasion, he told me matter-of-factly that if he found them, he would make them pay. I loved my dad; I begged him not to do anything he would regret. What would happen to us kids if he went to jail?

Those were some of my childhood's hardest days, but knowing I had a heavenly Father gave me the inner peace that comes with knowing I was never alone. I knew that the strength and courage to overcome the torment I was going through could come only from God.

My mom's drinking continued to get worse over the years. As we all got older, we found it more difficult to put up with all the abuse that was getting worse along with heavier drinking. All the love she once had for her family had turned into hate and resentment. We had to hide all the weapons in our house from her. She thought nothing of using violence against her children. When things got bad, we would run through the field jumping over terrace rows and hoping she was too drunk to catch us. In the summers, our cornfield was a great place to hide. Once we reached it and she couldn't see us anymore, she would shout a few choice words and get back to her drinking.

Without graphically describing the atrocities my mother inflicted on her children, I will simply say our home was a war zone for years. My dad never considered leaving because he didn't want to separate us kids. He felt that all we had was each other.

5
My Sanctuary above It All

Over the years, I began to trust that God's love was unconditional. God saw a willing vessel in me, someone with a heart that would sing his praises for life. I had been born into a poor family with limited means to change my life, but I knew that by giving my heart to God, I would be adopted by the King.

I had an overwhelming desire to learn more about God and Jesus. I passionately wanted to feed the Spirit who lived in me, but my parents never took me to church. It was left up to me to embark on my own spiritual journey, but having God's Spirit in me gave me all the love and peace I needed. God's Spirit will bring serenity into your life when everything else is in chaos.

A little Baptist church was about a mile from my house. I made a path through the woods there, and I would go as often as I could. I never feared the walk to church because I knew in my heart God had assigned me a guardian angel who would provide a hedge of protection for me. I attended other churches besides that one; it didn't matter to me what denomination a church had written on its exterior. I knew it was God's house, and that's whom I went to worship. My relationship with God was the same no matter where I went to church.

I eventually learned about a church that provided

transportation to and from worship, and one of my older brothers started attending church with me. The more I attended, the more I fell in love with Jesus. On more than one occasion, I felt his presence and knew he was with me; he never failed to be at my side in my times of need. I had learned about God's many promises and had learned to take him at his word. I had to deal with lies and deception at home, but God's Word, the Bible, was always true; I could always depend on it.

God promised he would never leave us or forsake us, and his promises gave me great hope; I believed his every word. At age nine, I made a commitment to God; I asked him to come into my heart to live there forever. I was baptized along with one of my older brothers. By being baptized, I was making a statement to the world that I was committed to God and he was permanently living in my heart.

The days leading up to my baptism were so exciting. I was bursting with anticipation, and having my brother baptized with me was the most exciting thing that had ever happened to me. Life would never be the same for my brother and me. The world would know that we had a heavenly Father and that we no longer felt the restraint of our humble beginnings. We looked forward to living the lives God had planned for us. My brother and I had faith that our heavenly Father would be our peace in times of trouble, our safe harbor in our storms of life, and our strength for the journey ahead.

God had seen the potential in us and our desire to become who he wanted us to be. Our parents didn't come to the service that night, but my mom made me a pretty dress out of a feed sack and some other scrap material. Though she ran out of material before she could put sleeves on it, I felt like a princess who had just been adopted by a King.

As the years went by, I had to take on more and more responsibilities with the addition of three more siblings—two girls and a sweet little brother. I promised myself that somehow, someday, I would shield my younger siblings from the emotional pain and disappointment my four older brothers and I had experienced. I always made sure they were fed and bathed. In the summer, I'd put them in the wagon along with a bottle of dish soap, haul them down to the creek, and sit each of them in a pothole. I gave them all bubble baths to clean them from head to toe. We shared the creek with frogs, spring lizards, and crawdads. Snakes along the shore and a few water moccasins were the only things I had to watch out for. A crawdad would occasionally get in my little sister's hair and she would pitch a hissy fit; she'd dance up and down the creek until I was able to rescue her from what she called a horrible creature.

But I couldn't protect them from everything. The younger children were in just as much danger as were we older children when mama started drinking. On more than one occasion, I had to tuck my younger siblings behind terrace rows or hide them in the cornfield.

I have fond memories of being the older sister to the three young 'uns. At times, my dad would take us to work with him cutting timber. He would stop by the general store to get supplies for the day, and our treat was to pick a dime's worth of penny candy out of the display case in our own little paper bags, which we called pokes. My dad would also pick up some bologna cut from a roll and a loaf of bread.

I was in charge of caring for the young 'uns; I made sure they were fed and kept dry. My dad would use twine to tie us to the nearest stump especially if there was any water nearby such as a creek or pond. That way, he knew we wouldn't be hit by a falling tree or drown. He felt better about us being by the water, where we could fish for our supper. My dad always let me have just enough slack in my line so I could reach the water's edge. I kept the baby bottles and milk cool and was able to wash my siblings' diapers slightly downstream and then dry them in the sun.

We also entertained ourselves by catching lightning bugs—fireflies—and an occasional turtle. Our favorite turtles were terrapin. They were small enough for us to handle, and we would turn them upside down on an old stump to make sure they would be there the next day.

One day, my dad was cutting timber on Cherry Mountain; my sister and I had been hanging out with him all day. We left our turtle upside down along with my sister's doll. Someone had given my sister the doll, and she had named it Walleye because it had only one eye. We didn't expect it to snow overnight, but when it did, my sister and I were very upset. She loved that baby doll and was afraid it would be buried in the snow along with our turtle friend. Being the person he was, my dad saddled up one of the horses and rode out in the snow to rescue our friend and bring Walleye home. After that, he scolded us if he saw us leaving another turtle upside down.

I loved going to work with my dad because in the woods, I saw all God's beauty and heard nature's sounds. It was a time of peace and contentment.

I found that being number five of eight children only meant I existed while trying to survive. My sanctuary was on top of our old barn. My brother and I built a ladder up the side of an old oak beside the barn with scraps of wood and some old, rusty, catawampus—crooked—nails we straightened out with a rock and a hammer.

I would climb the tree up to the top of the barn to enjoy my own space. I spent hours in my happy place there talking to God and creating things out of clay I'd gathered from the creek, then dried my creations in the sun. We never had toys, so I was always using my imagination to create different things.

I felt as close to heaven as I could get on the barn roof, and the more time I spent there, the closer I felt to God. There, I felt joy, not sadness. Talking to God gave me faith that someday, things would be better.

6 Honoring a Servant of God

When I was fourteen, God put another great person in my life. A classmate invited me to a girls' meeting on a Tuesday night at a Holiness Church. I met a woman who eventually became my second mother. She was a petite woman with a heart bigger than herself. She was a spirit-filled, godly woman who loved God and others as only she could. She was a fun-loving person who loved to make others smile.

I was so blessed to have this woman take me under her wing when I was at a vulnerable age and needed Christian guidance. She always made sure I had a ride to church even if that meant splashing her clean car down our muddy driveway through the puddles. Occasionally, she invited me over for Sunday dinner. She was an awesome cook, and she gave me some great culinary lessons. I always envied her daughter for having such a wonderful mother who was so full of love and kindness for everyone.

She taught me many things about shopping, cooking, and keeping a clean house that I hadn't learned at home. Pretty much anything she was fixin' to do—that is, about to do—she used as an opportunity to teach me another skill. She always had an understanding ear when I was facing one of those hardships associated with the teenage years. She would give me sound advice from a Christian perspective or provide a shoulder for me to cry on. She always made me feel that I could show up at her door anytime day or night.

But teenage years are hard even if you have great role models you can depend on. I loved my mom, but I refused to model myself after her because she had turned into someone who was so far from what I wanted to model myself after. Through this woman's loving guidance, I begin to realize I could become anything I wanted through hard work and education. It was a very eye-opening experience to learn firsthand how much easier life was when you had modern conveniences such as electricity and running water in your home.

Our friendship grew over the years. She and her husband were a big part of my life. They would invite me to go camping and show me places beyond my old shack. She was always a great example of what a parent should be. Along with discipline, she gave me a lot of love and respect. She always had plenty of hugs to go around, and she always made sure there was enough food on her table for unexpected guests. She'd say, "Just let me put another tater-potato-in the pot."

Everyone was sad when God called his angel home in 1997. Her legacy lives on in the lives she touched, and her testimony is the gratitude those individuals will carry with them for their whole lives. She was in the hospital for the last few days of her life. She was dependent on oxygen, but she was a giver; she felt it was more important to share God with others to her last breath than it was to die in silence. She was shouting and praising God like I'd never seen, and she was so sick! She had taken her oxygen mask off, and I felt as if I were at a camp meeting or a revival though we were right there in her room. She was from a large family, and she wanted to confirm to us all that Jesus was real. Being able to watch her journey to heaven was a beautiful experience. The Bible teaches us that to be absent from our bodies means we are present with God. Though my heart was broken, I knew she was singing with a choir of angels free from pain and sickness.

Throughout the years, I have received blessings, witnessed miracles, and experienced the freedom that comes with forgiveness because I was introduced to that loving servant of God. When life would throw me a curve ball, she would remind me that the Bible teaches us that if we have faith the size of a mustard seed, the smallest of all seeds, we can move mountains; all we have to do is simply believe. She proved that to me on more than one occasion, but I have discovered over the years that it was much easier for me to have faith when things were going great than it was when the chips were down and I was facing difficulties.

When we experience our inevitable trials in life, we need to stay focused on the lily that blooms in the valley whose name is Jesus. He will walk beside us and give us strength to walk out of the valley victoriously.

7
The Great Physician

When I was in the eighth grade, my mom suffered two brain aneurysms. She was put in the neuro intensive care unit at a nearby hospital. After stabilizing my mom enough for surgery, the doctor explained to our family that there was a fifty-fifty chance she wouldn't survive, and if she did, she'd face numerous complications.

He explained that they would have to remove a section of her skull to access and repair the two blood vessels that had ruptured. I knew God was the one, true Great Physician, and through prayer, I put my mom in his hands. I prayed night and day that God would guide the doctors' hands during surgery. I may not have agreed with some of the life choices my mom had made, but we all still loved and needed her. We hated the way she was under the influence of alcohol but not the person she really was.

I never left the waiting room during the ten hours she was in surgery. I saw the stress and worry on my dad's face. My mom had already been in the hospital for a week, and because the surgery was so complex, the hospital wanted to be able to reach someone for the next twelve days to make decisions on her behalf if complications arose.

In the 1970s, our family of course did not have cell phones, and because my dad was self-employed, that would be a major hardship on the family. He had an enormous amount of pride that would never allow him to ask for any help. His attitude was simply, "If we can't afford it, we can do without it." The essentials were food and shelter, and my dad always managed to provide at least that. But he was adding one more thing to the essentials list—hospital bills.

We spent ten hours in the hospital waiting room before the neurosurgeon came out to speak with my dad. My dad was wearing his well-worn overalls, and as the doctor shook his hand, he could tell by my dad's strong grip and calluses that he was no stranger to hard work. The doctor said that the surgery had been a success and that my mom would soon be out of recovery and back in her room.

During their conversation, the doctor asked my dad what he did for a living. My dad replied that he cut timber. The doctor said he needed a load of locust posts for a pasture fence on his farm. My dad was grateful for the work and told the doctor he would be glad to deliver a load of posts.

My mom stayed in the hospital for the next three weeks. My dad along with some of us children delivered a load of locust posts for the doctor's pasture. Soon, Mom was out of the hospital but not without a few reminders of just how serious her condition had been. The right side of her body had been affected; she was blind in one eye and had no feeling in her right foot. All she had ever done besides raising us kids was work at the textile mill.

We serve a God who can do awesome things. I had the utmost confidence God would deliver Mom back to us alive and in good health; we just had to believe. My dad had never been in debt to anyone for this amount of money; I could tell that the stress of not knowing where he would get the money to pay the medical bills worried him extremely.

But God took care of the hospital bill. After my dad delivered that load of posts, God put compassion in the surgeon's heart for us. When we got the hospital bill, it was marked paid in full. My dad called the hospital to question the bill believing that there had been a mistake; we hadn't applied for any kind of assistance. Whomever he spoke to insisted the bill had all been taken care of. All we could do as a family was break down and cry. God's grace is simply amazing. When we are limited, our God is unlimited.

I believed more than ever that my mom would eventually be able to see with both eyes and feel her right foot again. I prayed for a miracle but knew it would be in God's timing, not mine.

A few months later, my mom woke up one morning and so did her eye and foot. We rejoiced as a family and praised God for his awesomeness. My mom made a full recovery and went back to work.

I never get tired of hearing about the miracles God blesses people with. I have learned to depend on my friend, Jesus, for everything. He lived in my heart and was my safe harbor when the storms of life crashed against the shores of my soul.

8
The Blessing of Ability

God blessed me with the physical ability and desire to work hard every day, and I have. As far back as I can remember, I knew where the garden tools were and how to use them. From sunup to sundown on our farm, we needed to handle many chores to sustain ourselves. It took all the able-bodied members of our family to stay ahead.

I was so proud when I turned sixteen and started working at my mom's textile mill, which turned raw cotton into fabric and employed many in our county. We worked from 4:00 p.m. to midnight, so when I got out of school at 1:00, I rode the early school bus to a stop sign about a mile from the shack. I ran down the trail I used to get to church as a child to catch a ride to work with my mom.

My life started to change. I was getting my own paycheck—$98 a week—and that meant I could finally protect my younger siblings from the shame, humiliation, and disappointment I had felt as a child going to school. For my whole life, I had been looked down upon and made fun of for the way I had to dress. I was told many times that I would never amount to a hill of beans. With my paycheck, I was determined to prove them wrong. I bought my younger siblings clothes and good, name-brand shoes. And when the holidays rolled around, there was always something under the tree for each of them.

One of my older brothers started working at the factory also, and he and I bought nice things for the younger kids including toy trucks, bicycles, and baby dolls, things we had never had as children; we did that for the simple pleasure of seeing them smile. I smiled when I thought the young 'uns would never be made fun of for the clothes or shoes they wore. Because we hadn't had much growing up, anything we worked for meant the world to us, and we felt very blessed.

I have always believed in premonitions and visions though it isn't always clear to me which one I'm having at any one time. We lived some ways out of town, and no one in our area thought anything about leaving a window or door open for a cool breeze in the summer even if we weren't home.

One of my brothers had moved into a shack not far from where we were raised. He bought a shotgun not long after moving there. One day while he was at work, someone stole his new gun. He had worked hard to buy it, and it wasn't likely he'd be able to purchase another one anytime soon. He was very upset and called the police to report it stolen. The police filed a report but weren't able to do much more than that.

I was still living at home, and all my money was helping support the family, so I turned to my friend, Jesus, for help. I got on my knees and prayed that God would convict the heart of the person who had taken the shotgun and that he would return it. That night, God gave me a vision that revealed to me that the gun would be returned and how the person would return it.

The next morning, I shared the vision with my mom; I had been shown a man in a light-colored car bringing the shotgun back to our home rather than my brother's. The gun would be in the trunk of the man's car covered with a yellow towel, and he would bring the shotgun into the house and set it by the bedroom door. In my vision, I noticed that the person who had taken the gun had tried to change its identity by carving something on the stock.

I was so excited that my brother would get his shotgun back that it never entered my mind that it wouldn't happen. At midday, the front door of our shack was open to let fresh air in. My mom was sitting on the couch embroidering, and I was doing something in the kitchen when a car came up the driveway. There was something familiar about the car, but I couldn't quite place it. Then it dawned on me—it was the car from my vision. I was excited that my vision was unfolding in front of my eyes. This would be a great testimony about what an awesome God we serve.

Sure enough, the man got out of the car and retrieved the gun, which was wrapped in a yellow towel, from the trunk. I said, "Look, Mom! Here comes the man. He'll set the gun by the bedroom door."

The man did exactly that. He apologized for his actions and said that he couldn't live with himself; he said he felt convicted to return the shotgun. I thanked God for the man's conviction. Taking full advantage of the lesson I was hopefully getting through to my mom, I told her to lift the towel and she would see some carving on the stock.

I always tried to witness to my mom in hopes she would begin to praise God as she had earlier in her life. I never quit believing that someday, somehow, God would break the bond that was preventing her from being the loving, nurturing person she once had been.

I had read God's promises; I knew that his love was the same love parents had for their children and that he would give me the strength to protect myself if I was ever in danger.

9
In the Name of Jesus

In our house, guns were always loaded. We learned at an early age that guns were not toys, that we had to treat them with respect. We also learned that guns were for gathering food and for our protection.

One day, I was watching the three young 'uns and we heard a noise in a bedroom. Not knowing what to expect, I grabbed the shotgun that was propped against the wall next to Haskell and went rushing into the room with my three little siblings tucked in behind me like train cars with the caboose being the youngest, my baby brother.

A man was trying to climb through the open window. I knew he wasn't coming to visit, so I marched right up to him, stuck the shotgun hard up against his nose, and commanded, "In the name of Jesus leave us alone!"

The man's eyes were firmly crossed staring at the barrel of the shotgun as he slowly slithered out the window. We heard his heavy footsteps as he ran away from the shack. I know in my heart that Jesus had given me strength to face that intruder.

I had never shot a gun as big as the shotgun before. Later, after the adrenaline wore off and we realized we were out of danger, we all had a good laugh about the domino effect the recoil would have had on all four of us if I had fired it. The young 'uns had witnessed firsthand the strength that comes from within when you believe in God and his protection.

I had another opportunity to witness the power in Jesus's name when one of my brothers and I decided to surprise our mom with something to make her life a little easier—we bought her a matching electric range and refrigerator. The only experience I had operating an electric range was with the woman who had taken me under her wing and was gently preparing me for a life beyond the shack.

As we were awaiting delivery of the appliances, we were so excited to be doing something of that magnitude that we had overlooked an important detail—the appliances needed to be plugged up, as we said, to an electrical outlet, and there weren't any in the shack. The only electricity we had ran to the lightbulbs in the ceiling. But we called an electrician to install some outlets.

Once we got the appliances hooked up, we felt we had advanced into the modern age. The first meal I attempted to prepare for the young 'uns on the new stove was a familiar one; I thought this was going to be the easiest batch of potatoes I'd ever prepared. I peeled and cut up the potatoes and heated up some lard in our old cast-iron pan on the front burner on high. I was impressed at the ease with which it was all coming together. I was so happy just to turn a knob to the high position and watch the elements turn red hot.

One of my older brothers had started dating and had installed a phone in the shack. When the phone rang, I was so excited to answer it and be connected to a world beyond our shack that I completely forgot about the pan full of cooking lard. When I returned to the kitchen, all I could see was a wall of flames.

Our shack was made of pine boards, and with no sheetrock on the ceilings, there was nothing between those flames and the pine rafters. If our house burned down, we would have been homeless. I called on Jesus. The flames were too high for me to get near the stove and turn the burner off. But Jesus had never let me down before, and I had no reason to believe he would let me down then.

I saw fear in my little brother's face, and I knew it was now or never. I told him to stand back; I said help was on its way. I raised my hands and said in a clear, commanding voice, "In the name of Jesus, quench that fire." The flames immediately subsided, and I wrapped a rag around the handle of the pan. With both hands firmly around the handle, I carried it outside careful not to spill any of the cooking lard left in it. I was grateful but not surprised that my friend, Jesus, had come to my aid upon my cries for help. The flame had gone out so suddenly in the name of Jesus that it was as if God had put a lid on the pan.

God reconfirmed his love for me that day, and I will always sing his praises. My younger siblings had witnessed a prayer being answered right in front of them. Believing in something you can't see or touch is hard especially when you're young. My faith has been tested on numerous occasions but never to that magnitude. Faith and the power in Jesus's name had quenched the fire.

The most important thing to me was that my siblings witnessed my crying out to Jesus; that caused a miracle. They have never forgotten that day, and they have developed their own relationships with God. They learned that God hears our cries for help in our times of trouble and that we can always count on the power in Jesus's name.

10
Christmas on Cherry Mountain

From the decorations to the pretty twinkling lights, there is a special feeling in the air at Christmas, a beautiful time of year. The scars I had from my childhood disappointments at Christmas were replaced by the joy of giving. I found it hard to talk about Christmas even after I had a job and was able to bring joy and happiness to the less fortunate.

I love the hustle and bustle of the season. As a child, I heard stories at school and church about houses decorated for Christmas and trees with ornaments in the living room; I knew about Santa coming down the chimney with gifts and stockings filled to the brim with candy and treats hanging over the fireplace. I heard about families gathered around their trees singing Christmas songs about Jesus and the beautiful celebration of the season.

Outside our home, all these things seemed real, but at our house, Christmas was different. The treats we kids received came from a bag of goodies my mom received from her place of employment. We were thankful to get the treats because we rarely got apples, oranges, or orange slice candy. The holiday season for my mom was drowned by the effects of moonshine. My dad didn't have the money to bring gifts to us all, so he was very sad during the holidays.

I don't remember a tree being set up in our house until I was in first grade and began thinking about how to get Santa to stop at my house. We needed a Christmas tree and a fireplace I thought. I knew we wouldn't get a fireplace, but other kids at school didn't have fireplaces and they still got Christmas presents. I thought I could change Christmas at our house by simply getting a tree. I brought home a gallon bucket from the school cafeteria and asked my dad if we could put a small tree in it.

From then on, as a family, we would go into the woods on our property and my dad would chop down a small cedar tree. We would put rocks in the bucket to help stand the tree up, and we sat the bucket in the living room even if we had to tie the tree to the wall with string around a nail to make it stand up. We decorated our tree with popcorn we would string.

Christmas came; once again, Santa hadn't stopped to see our Christmas tree or leave any presents under it. I started asking more questions at school and learned that I needed to write a letter to Santa about what I wanted. One other thing I found out was that I had to be a good girl. I figured that would be easy because I was already a good girl. I almost always made A's in school and always honored my parents just as the Bible told me to do. I always did my chores and my homework.

The next Christmas, I thought I had done everything right. Imagine my disappointment trying to grasp why Santa, who traveled the world on Christmas Eve leaving toys for boys and girls, forgot to stop by my house again though we had a Christmas tree and I had written Santa a nice letter explaining how good we all had been and what exactly we wanted for Christmas. We were so sad and hurt that we went to bed with our broken hearts hugging are pillows tight crying ourselves to sleep. We wondered what was wrong with us that had caused Santa to simply pass us by.

It was hard going to school after the Christmas holidays

because when it was time for show and tell, I had to decide if I would tell the truth about not receiving gifts or tell a lie, which was against my principles, and pretend I fit in with the other kids who were telling stories about the toys they'd found under their trees on Christmas morning.

The one thing I'll never forget about Christmas was the circumstances in which Jesus was born. Because I had also born in humble surroundings, I felt a kinship with Jesus; I knew that he was real, someone I could believe in, and that he would never let me down and leave me disappointed as Santa had done year after year. Jesus would always be the one true gift God gave the world. Remembering the real reason for the season didn't take all the pain and disappointment away from the holiday though the season was beautiful. But the whole other side of Christmas left me with deep emotional scars.

I was glad to learn the truth about Santa; that gave me the strength I needed to put smiles on children's faces at Christmas. My older brothers and I always sheltered the young 'uns at Christmas and made sure they never cried themselves to sleep thinking Santa had forgotten them.

No matter how many hours I had to work to make it possible, Santa never again forgot to stop at our house on Christmas Eve. It was so rewarding to see the smiles on their little faces knowing they were loved. They could enjoy the holiday season like other children with presents under the tree on Christmas morning.

11
Like a Butterfly

The day arrived that I had been dreaming about for years. I turned eighteen, and like a butterfly, I finally shed my cocoon and fluttered out of my situation. From then on, I would make my own decisions and create my own path in life.

I had to make some tough decisions. I knew I would have to work hard to support myself and save up enough for a car. I hadn't had a reason to get a driver's license, so I needed to start working on that as well.

I rented a room close to where I was working so I could walk to work. My room was closer to a sawmill than it was to the textile mill, so I switched jobs. It paid the same as the textile mill, but the work was a lot harder. I was thankful I had been raised like the boys and had helped my dad cut timber; I wasn't a stranger to hard work.

I saw my dad regularly; he would deliver loads of logs to the sawmill and often bring me lunch. He would have a cold drink and some Beanie Weenies in his pocket for me. He was glad to see me becoming an independent woman able to leave that old shack I'd called home.

He knew I needed a car, so he gave me driving lessons on the weekends. I'd driven farming equipment, but driving on city streets would take some getting used to, but it wasn't long before

I was ready to take my driving test. My dad took me to take the test, and when I passed it, before the ink was dry on my license, he told me he would cosign a loan so I could buy a car. Because I had transportation, I no longer needed to work at the sawmill. I was tired of constantly being bruised and pulling muscles from handling lumber all day, so I applied for a job at the textile mill, and they were glad to have me back.

I lived the way I felt God wanted me to. I always included God in all my life decisions. I worked at several jobs and in different locations through the years always trying to improve myself. In my early twenties, I married a local man with a Christian background and deep family roots.

One miracle I was blessed with didn't start out as a miracle at all. I was presented with the paralyzing reality that I had inherited polycystic ovary disease from my mom's side. My disease was isolated in my ovaries; doctors told me I had only a slim chance of having children. My ovaries were three times the average size. A doctor suggested surgery, but the risks involved were more than I was willing to take. The only chance I had to beat this disease would come from the Great Physician. A great man of God had led the church I'd been a member of since I was fourteen. He never missed an opportunity to preach his heart out about what a wonderful God we served. He was filled with the Holy Spirit, and I had seen great things happen at our church around that old altar. God's power would be so real that it felt God himself was in our midst. I laid anything I ever needed to at the foot of that old altar.

The church had a group of wonderful prayer warriors who prayed for whatever was brought to their attention. The Bible teaches us to pray without ceasing; doing that along with believing while holding onto our faith is all we can do. Our prayers are not always answered in our timing, but they are answered in God's perfect timing. We can't see beyond our problems; only God has the big picture, and he holds our future in his hands.

I witnessed the Spirit of God descend upon this great man of God. I stood reverently as he spoke in tongues and prophesied. I yearned for the relationship with God he had. Once he had given his sermon, it was time for the altar call. Our preacher would look over the congregation and make a reference to an ailment or a specific problem he felt someone was struggling with. He looked straight at me and said, "Someone here is in need of the Great Physician."

I answered the call; I headed straight for the altar expecting a miracle. I had never explained my need to the pastor, but God knew my heart. I asked God for a son that day, and while I was on my knees, the pastor laid his hands on me and gave me a message straight from God: "When the timing is right, I will give you the desires of thy heart." I took God at his word; three years later, I got pregnant with my first son. The gynecologist asked what fertility drugs I had been using. He said that medically, it was nearly impossible for me to have gotten pregnant because my ovaries where three times the normal size. I had been told at the time of my original diagnosis that by the time I was twenty-eight, I would have to have them removed.

My son brought us such joy; he was a true gift from God. A couple years later I had a second son, and again, I felt so blessed. They were healthy, strapping boys. When I went back for my six-week checkup, I told my doctor that if I still needed that surgery, I would be okay with that; I felt two children were all I needed. I knew a healing miracle had taken place between the birth of my two sons because the look on the doctor's face was one of overwhelming surprise. He told me my ovaries were clear and of normal size.

That was in the late eighties. Thirty years later, I had to have a hysterectomy due to severe anemia. I told the surgeon to take whatever she felt necessary to ensure my health. Not surprisingly, she elected to leave me with my ovaries because they were still in perfect condition. When the healing is a gift from God, there won't be any difference between what your body would be normally and what it is after the healing.

A word of advice—let's not forget to give our children to God and teach them where their true help comes from and to always live by faith, not by sight. Children live by example, so take yours to church if at all possible and live the life you want them to live. Teach them about God and to pray when they face struggles. This is where our help and strength come from; it's a power greater than anything on earth. Teach them they have a heavenly Father who watches over them and is just a whisper away. We always wonder as they are growing up if they are really paying attention when we are taking them to church.

For years, one of my sons dealt with ADHD. We tried medicine and watched his diet, but nothing seemed to work. We would study spelling words with him, and he could spell every word back to us perfectly, but when put in a classroom environment to take a test, he would get only about 40 percent of the words correct. That was so discouraging.

When he was in sixth grade, I was working late into the evenings and my husband worked the night shift. We employed a child care provider after school to care for the boys and help them with their homework. When it came time for end-of-grade testing, my son with ADHD was devastated by something the person we were paying to help him with his homework said; she told him a snowball had a better chance of making it across the Sahara Desert than he had of passing his tests.

When I got home from work, he asked me, "Mom, I want you to pray with me about taking my test tomorrow." Though I could tell he was discouraged because of that care provider's statement, I asked him if he had done his part by studying for the test. I said, "If we do our part, I'm sure God will do his."

We knelt and asked God to help him remember what he

had learned. He had faith he would do well on his test because he believed God would do his part. The next day after school, he excitedly told me that the snowball had made it all the way across the Sahara; he had successfully passed the end-of-grade testing. It was heartwarming to know that at such a young age, my son knew exactly where his true help came from. God helped him with his studies so he could pass that test, and he also healed him of ADHD.

I have witnessed my son growing up into a young man and have seen him accomplish so much after he was healed of ADHD. He is now an accomplished rotor and fixed-wing pilot with a list of additional ratings and accomplishments as long as his arm. I am proud of all his accomplishments.

12 Building My First Pulpit

In the late eighties, I started getting feelings I couldn't shake, feelings that I was supposed to be doing something with my life other than what I was doing. Working in the textile industry was a job, but I had little interaction with people. When God saved me, he gave me a love for people, so that part of my life was missing.

I started praying for his guidance. The answer I got from God's Spirit was telling me to go to cosmetology school. The message was clear, but I didn't have the confidence to make such a commitment at that time. I asked God, "Am I hearing you correctly? Cosmetology school?" I would be dealing with the very public that all my life was convinced I wouldn't amount to a hill of beans. I had no self-confidence and no self-esteem. It's not that I doubted God's word; I just wanted to make sure I was receiving the message correctly.

But God knows us better than we know ourselves, so I told my husband about the direction I wanted to take. Losing half our income while raising our two boys and other responsibilities wouldn't be easy, but my husband was a good Christian man, and I knew that if God wanted me to do this, he would support me in my decision.

When I gave my life to Christ and asked him to give me

a servant's heart, I meant every word, but that doesn't make obedience any easier. I couldn't see at the time why it was so important to God for me to change direction and pursue a life in cosmetology, but I enrolled in the cosmetology program at our local college.

This decision wasn't going to come without serious sacrifices for my family, but I trusted God and knew he would provide for all our needs just as he had all my life. I started working out a budget for our family of four to live on—$289 a week. My husband's entire paycheck one week went to pay for my kit and books I needed for class—my first week of school and I had already blown my budget. I began to question my decision. I had never doubted my ability to read what I believed to be God speaking to my heart, but I had never made a commitment of that magnitude strictly on faith before either.

I got on my knees and prayed for guidance expecting to hear God tell me I had misunderstood him, but the message remained the same. God spoke to my heart; he told me that I was doing his work and that I should continue my schooling. I went back to the budget and reworked my numbers; that meant even more sacrifices for the family. Child care was a huge portion of the budget, but there wasn't any cutting I could do there.

When I returned to school the next day, my instructor told me he had been so impressed with my first four days in school that I would advance to the lab the next day. I knew that eventually I would need uniforms for working in the lab on people's hair, but I hadn't realized it would be so soon. I didn't have the money then to spend on a uniform, so I prayed, "Okay, God, what do I do now"? But God already had a plan and answered before the end of the day by sending a woman over to me who was about my size and height. She said, "I'm graduating and was wondering if you would like to have my uniforms." My eyes watered with relief and gratitude as I graciously accepted the gift.

The school uniform was whites, so all I had to do was bleach them out and they looked brand new. After that, I didn't doubt I had heard God correctly and was doing what he wanted me to do. God blessed my talent, and I went on enjoying my classes, winning various awards, and making the dean's list every quarter. I was so happy to be doing God's work that I developed a boldness and began to have confidence in my abilities.

Before I was able to finish cosmetology school, my dad became very ill. He was never one to complain or visit a doctor. He believed in home remedies, so when he told me to take him to the hospital, I knew something was really wrong. My dad was so important to me. School would always be there, but not my dad. I took a leave of absence from school so I could care for him. I took him to the hospital; he was very thin and not himself. He was grateful I was with him because he trusted me to make the right decisions for him.

After a day of testing, the doctor told us he was in the advanced stages of lung cancer that had spread. That was one of the hardest days of my life; I felt helpless seeing my hero so sick. I prayed for God to give me strength.

Dad spent the next five weeks in the hospital before he started asking to go home. With the help of hospice care and his sons and daughters taking turns caring for him, we were able to grant him that wish. I used what little time he had left to talk about his life. He told me during our talks that he had cried as many tears as I had when I didn't get a doll I'd wanted for Christmas. Knowing my dad and his heart made of gold, I'm sure he did.

He also told me something that would have changed everything in our lives. He told me about an opportunity he had had that would have ended the lives of my mother and her boyfriend. He told me he was once driving a logging truck full of logs behind my mother and her boyfriend. He was so enraged that he tailgated the two of them for several minutes contemplating ramming the logging truck into the back of their car. He was so engulfed in the situation that he had completely forgotten that my sister and I were in the truck with him. As he contemplated his next move, he happened to look over at his dirty-faced little girls sleeping beside him. We had been working in the woods with him all day. He realized at that moment that his children's live were more important than his emotions at the moment. Once again, his selflessness shined through and love prevailed over hate.

He had the opportunity to tell everyone goodbye. He thanked his friends for the kindness they had shown our family through the years. He even sent for a man he had once had harsh words with to ask for his forgiveness.

One day during that week, he told me about a dream he had had the night before. He told me that my sister who had passed away when she was just three months old thirty-nine years previously had visited him in his dream. He described her as a beautiful young woman with a robe so white that it looked iridescent. She told him that if he came with her, he would never be sick again. He said he told her to let him tell her brothers and sisters goodbye; when she came back, he would be ready to go with her.

He started preparing by getting me to cut his hair and shave him. It was hard to do when a man who had once stood six foot two was a skeleton at seventy-two pounds. It was as if he were preparing for his journey to heaven. He sent for the pastor to help him prepare for his daughter's return. He was at peace and showed no fear while he was preparing to make his journey home. But I was preparing myself for the most unimaginable pain of losing my hero. I knew God would have to carry me because I didn't have the strength to walk that path alone.

When I got up on Sunday morning, I had a feeling I couldn't explain. I told my husband that I felt as if I had a coat on. I felt its presence but didn't see it. God had wrapped me in a coat of his love and grace.

On Sunday night, I stayed with Dad until 11:00. His breathing had gotten worse, but he never complained. My sister came to spend the night with him so I could handle some chores that had been piling up. At home, I received that dreadful call. My sister said she had called an ambulance to take Dad to the hospital. I asked God to let me talk to him just once more. I had left out one important thing in our talks, and I was praying for the opportunity to tell him that.

After they got him settled in the emergency room, his family gathered around his bed. He motioned with his hand for me to come closer since he had no breath to speak out loud. He whispered that he was going home, and he tried to show me what he could see. He was pointing at the ceiling with his eyes focused on heaven. I knew he saw my sister returning to take him home. That was the chance I had prayed for. I told him he had been the best dad in the whole world, and I told him to go be at rest.

I was always afraid of death until that night. Then, I realized how easy crossing over from one life to the next can be. God was listening to me that night when I was driving to the hospital; the paramedics said they had lost my dad three times en route to the hospital.

The next morning, we drove to my brother's house to tell him Dad had passed away. He didn't have a telephone, so we hadn't had a way to contact him any earlier. He wasn't surprised at all. He shared what had happened to him during the night that let him know Dad was gone. He knew the exact time of dad's passing without our telling him. I believe my dad was trying to show me what God was allowing my brother to see from miles away. My brother said it was almost like a dream, but he was awake. We were amazed to hear that in his vision, he had seen

Dad at the hospital though no one had told him the ambulance had transported him during the night.

He said the clock had read 4:30 a.m., the time my dad passed away. He said he saw six angels come down and stand around dad's hospital bed. When the angels ascended to heaven, he saw two dads; one was with the angels and the other remained in the bed. That was a beautiful confirmation that my dad was in heaven.

I made the funeral arrangements, and we received over 600 friends the next night at the funeral home. The next day, we buried my dad at the cemetery beside an empty grave site reserved for his wife of forty years and the daughter they had lost and buried years earlier. It was amazing how much strength and courage I had wearing my coat of God's grace. I thank God every day that he is mindful of what his children are going through.

After all the ceremonies were over, I woke up one morning and my coat was gone. I was free to return to school and finish my cosmetology degree.

As it turned out, God gave me a boldness for talking to people, and I enjoyed having people sit in my chair every day. As I began to be more comfortable communicating with customers, I began to share God's love with them. That's when I realized that that had been God's plan all along. I had experienced firsthand God's love and protection growing up, and God had given me a pulpit from which I was to share those experiences with others.

I knew I was doing God's work, so I no longer had a confidence problem, and my skills improved with dedication and continued education. After graduating, I had to find a job. Most of the time, your school clients don't follow you to a salon. I said, "Okay, God, I've done everything you told me to do, so now, I need a job and a clientele."

Finding a job was easy. Many salons in our county rented

chairs and stations to hairdressers for a fixed rate per month. The owners of the salons would be paid the same whether a beautician had many clients or none, so it was entirely up to me to build a clientele. I had to supply all my tools and products I needed to make people beautiful, and that was very expensive.

Once again, I found myself on my knees asking God to help me make the right decisions for my family. God ensured me I was doing his work, and he told me to rent a booth at a salon in town. It wasn't a great location, but as it turned out, it was exactly where God wanted me to be.

I knew God never took us out on a limb and just left us there. If we do our part, God will do his. The day I was moving my things into the salon to start work, a woman came in for me to do her hair. She had heard good things about my performance in school and wanted to be my first customer. She was a blessing from God for all my hard work. She referred all her friends and coworkers to me. My hard work and faith in God paid off in the form of a wonderful clientele base. My career in cosmetology was designed by God to be my ministry.

But just as things were beginning to go smoothly, Satan showed up to try to destroy everything by exposing an allergy I had to the chemicals that affected my hands. The doctor said it was contact dermatitis; I had so many blisters on my hands that I was afraid I wouldn't be able to continue my career in cosmetology. The chemicals I used for work burned my hands so badly that taking a perm down or rinsing out color was unbearable. My hands would be bleeding, cracked, and blistered when I got home, and they would hurt and itch so much that I couldn't sleep. I would have to run cold water over my hands to get relief. But I told God that I was willing to stay in cosmetology and continue spreading his Word, but it would require another healing miracle and fast.

The doctor said I could wear gloves, but that wasn't the solution. I couldn't wear gloves for way too many things I had to do. Once again, I found myself at that old altar asking for a miracle; I gave my hands to God, and he healed my hands that day.

I still have a lot of allergies, one of which stops me from coloring my hair. I was convinced that would be a hindrance as I got older because professional cosmetologists are always required to look the part. But God blessed me with beautiful silver hair, and it has never been an issue.

After I had a significant clientele and was busy, God revealed the next stage of his master plan for me. He began to weigh on my heart to open up my own hair salon. I had never dreamed of owning my own business, but God began to send me unmistakable signals that pointed toward that. The strongest signals came from my clients; they were constantly asking me if I had ever thought about opening a salon myself. I knew that would require a miracle since I had developed yet another medical issue. And I would need each and every customer to pay the bills, so I wouldn't be able to call in sick.

I had been dealing with migraines that would last for days. Migraines are very debilitating due to the pain and sickness they cause. I wasn't taking any prescription medication, only what I could get over the counter because I didn't have medical insurance. I was sensitive to lights, sounds, and smells. I spent many nights in the bathroom because the pain was so great that it caused me to have diarrhea and vomiting. A cold, wet washcloth and prayer were all I could depend on for relief. If I were to open a salon, I knew I had to seriously talk to God if this was his plan for my life.

Our church had a revival coming up, and I planned on going. It was uplifting to attend revivals and get my spirit fed. I love gospel music and the feeling that comes with worshiping God.

On the first night of the revival, I was pulled between staying home to deal with a migraine I had had for three days or go to church. I decided to attend, and I thank God I did. That was my day for a miracle. It was a visiting pastor from Hickory, North Carolina. I didn't know him, but God did.

After the sermon, it was time for the altar call, and he looked straight at me and said, "Someone here has had a migraine for three days, and tonight is her night for healing. God has seen your suffering and wants to heal you." Not believing the healing was for me, I patiently waited on someone else to step out into the aisle. When I saw no one move, I stepped out and let the sweet Spirit of God lead me to the altar. Thank God I had been obedient. That was my night for healing. From that day forward, I never experienced another migraine.

Satan will whisper in our ears that we aren't worthy of God's blessings. If we let him, he will rob us of some of the greatest blessings God has in store for us, his children. That night convinced me God was preparing me for the next chapter of my life.

I was flattered that my clients had faith that I could open my own salon, but the fear that came along with the possibility of failure weighed heavily on my heart. New hair salons have one of the highest failure rates among businesses.

I didn't have any extra money, but I knew my urges were coming from God, so I began to investigate how I could pull this off. I was raising a family and had been a hairstylist for only a couple of years. The more I investigated, the more things started to happen. I even had a vision of where my salon was supposed to be. I saw the existing sign in my dream and recognized it. The realization that this might be possible began to sink in. The location in my dream was in a major shopping center and had 1,800 square feet of space. If not for my vivid vision, I would have looked for something far less grand. However, I knew in my heart that if this was God's plan, everything would fall into place.

I prayed that if this wasn't God's plan, "Please God, put stumbling blocks in my way." Stumbling blocks did indeed show up, but they never blocked my way for long; solutions accompanied every one of them. I went to the location I had seen in my vision to see if there was something to rent there, and I saw a For Rent sign in the window. True to my vision, it was for 1,800 square feet. I was sure this place was way out of reach, but out of curiosity, I met with the realtor who had the listing.

The realtor said that it normally rented for a lot but that because it has been on the market for so long, the owner wanted to get it rented, so the price would be much less. It was well within reason; I calculated that with just three booth renters, I could afford the rent.

The next expense I needed to determine was for utilities. Since I had never had commercial property in my name before, I wondered how that would be possible. I learned that the utility company required a substantial deposit from anyone who hadn't been in its system before. I prayed, "God, we've come this far. How do we proceed?"

God spoke to my heart; he told me to speak to a salon owner in a different shopping center. I thought, *Wow, God! You really must have a sense of humor. Why on earth would she possibly help me?* But being obedient, I made a haircut appointment for myself just to talk to her about my idea. I knew God would have to do all the talking because I didn't have a clue how to start a conversation about needing someone to cosign for my utilities. I had never asked anyone for anything in my life, but God was weighing heavy on my heart that this was what I was supposed to do. I didn't know the woman personally; she was only an acquaintance. I sat in her chair, and words started pouring out of my mouth, I couldn't believe I was speaking, but I told her all about my plans to open a salon, and to my surprise, she was so happy for me.

I never even had to ask for any help; she volunteered hers: "I'll be happy to help you with anything you need." I asked, "Are you sure?" She said yes. I said my biggest hurdle was the deposits on the utilities—$600 for water and $600 for electricity.

She told me to bring the paperwork by and she would be happy to cosign it. It was amazing watching God open every door one at a time. My husband was a plumber and his brother was an electrician. That left the painting up to me. All the pieces of the puzzle were in place except for the salon equipment. I had a credit card, but I wanted God to find another way for me to equip the salon.

That was the last stumbling block I faced. I was still working at the salon I had been working at for two years while I was doing all this research. When the sales representative for a beauty supply company came by the salon, I pulled him to the side and told him about my plan to open a salon. I asked him if there was any type of a ninety-day plan or if he had any promotions going on that might help me. I should've known God had that matter under control as well. The salesman said, "I'll get you the equipment, and I won't bill you for it until you can pay it in full."

All my research was complete. I gave the owner of the salon thirty days' notice, and my husband and I prepared for opening day. I opened on schedule but not before walking through the salon and dedicating every square inch to God's glory. All I needed at that point was customers and booth renters. Hard work wasn't going to be an issue; I just needed people sitting in my chair.

The salon was an instant success. It wasn't long before I had all my booths rented and customers filling all the chairs. I asked God every day to give me the right words to say to whoever sat in my chair.

God knows everyone's needs, and my goal was to speak with people from all walks of life in the hope I could introduce my friend, Jesus, to those with open ears and hearts. My job was clear—I would share my vision of hope and salvation. My salon station—my pulpit—was my way of giving back to God all he had given me. Sharing Jesus to each customer who sat in my chair became my life's work.

13
Finding Forgiveness

My mom had been saved at a young age and had grown up going to church. She would tell us kids about playing the guitar and singing God's praises. She knew what it was like to serve God, but Satan had managed to lure her from her faith with alcohol. Alcohol is like a thread; if you put your wrists together and let someone wrap thread around them a few times, you can still break free, but if enough thread is wrapped around, it will become a bond that is very hard to break. I knew only God could break the thread that held my mom in bondage, and I prayed endlessly for her salvation.

We should never give up on those we love. As long as we're breathing, we can hope for forgiveness, one of God's gifts to us. He offers us eternal life right up to our last breath; then, it's our choice where we spend eternity.

In the late eighties, my mom's health began to fail. She had inherited polycystic kidney disease from her dad. She was on a dialysis machine that acted as an artificial kidney; all her blood had to be filtered through this machine for several hours every other day. Her diet and fluid intake had to be closely monitored daily. The disease forced my mom to make some life-changing decisions.

Sometimes, we have to go through trials before we can wake

up from worldly things and realize we need help the world can't offer, help that comes only from God. I continued to pray for my mom and relentlessly encouraged her to go to church with me. My mom needed a Savior as well as a doctor. I knew that if she went to church and gave her life back to God, she would find peace. Our forgiving God looks beyond our faults and recognizes our needs.

She went on dialysis and maintained her health for the next few years. She gave up alcohol; that prayer was answered. More times than I cared to remember, I'd watched her transform from a loving, caring person to one with a heart full of hate and discontent. It was a beautiful journey to see a brand-new mom and what God could do. Our old mom, who used to fill us with uncertainty and fear, was gone. God restored the nurturing, loving person with a compassionate heart I had been praying for. God had broken the thread that once held her in bondage. She was free to live the rest of her life with her heart full of love for her family.

Ironically, the disease that was claiming her life had given her life back to her and was giving her time to prepare for her new life with God in heaven. I will always feel that God called my dad home before my mom so our family would be able to focus on the loving side of our mother, not the mother who had wasted so many years in bondage.

After my dad died, I was bitter at first; I selfishly believed my dad had been deprived of a few good years without the constant reminder that the woman he had embarked on the American Dream with had changed. I felt empty and even a little lost knowing I could never go to him when I was sick or in need of sound advice. I remained sad until God gave me a dream that revealed my dad in a beautiful place free of pain and sorrow. Seeing him smile removed the sadness from my heart. He told me not to worry about him; he said he was the happiest he had ever been. That was all I needed; I no longer dwelt on the emptiness I felt due to losing him.

I turned my focus to my mom; I forgave her, and I rekindled the love I once felt for her. I had never stopped loving my mom, but this love was deeper than the love I had hung onto over the years. Forgiveness is a beautiful thing. It gives us back our lives so we can move forward. Unforgiveness only destroyed me. It robbed me of my everyday joy and happiness and the full life God intended for me.

Satan uses this tool against us to make us see only the negatives, not the positives. I realized forgiveness was a gift I gave myself. God tells us in his Word that if we can't forgive others, he can't forgive us. The peace and joy that follows is amazing.

My mom struggled with kidney failure and heart disease. I prayed earnestly for her healing, but I knew healing of that magnitude could come only from God. I had experienced his healing in my life, and I knew God could easily heal her if it was his will. She was only in her fifties, so if she were in good health and no longer under the bondage of alcohol, she would be free to live out the rest of her years in peace with love in her heart.

As I prayed to God for her healing, God asked me, "If I answer your prayer, will she serve me?" I had to question my reason for so desperately wanting my mom to be healed. I honestly couldn't answer the obvious question. Since alcohol had been such a formidable opponent in her life, would she be able to live alcohol free or would she again fall prey to moonshine?

Not willing to lose my mom again, I prayed a different prayer—that God's will be done. I felt I would rather lose my mom in her fifties and heaven be her home than take a chance of losing her all over again to a life she once knew. Addiction is a powerful evil that only God can help us overcome. I believe we sometimes suffer afflictions to humble us and bring us closer to God. Thankfully, we serve a God who refuses to give up on us.

My mom started coming to church with me regularly, and I began thinking it wouldn't be as hard as I thought to let her go especially when I witnessed her at the altar with her hands lifted and praising God. She had made things right between God and herself. At that moment, I realized all was well with her soul. I gave her to God again that day. All I could say was, "God, it's your will, not mine."

Soon after I witnessed my mom praising God at church, she was admitted to the hospital. She was there for a week trying to get her health under control. I visited her often, but when Sunday came, I felt something was different about our visit; I felt God had designed that day just for us. It was Easter Sunday, the beautiful day when we celebrate our Savior's resurrection.

My mom had never been affectionate or sentimental; she was stern, and her personality had always appeared to be cold. It was as if she had a hard crust. I can't remember her ever saying "I love you." That might have been the result of her upbringing, or perhaps she hadn't learned to love herself and thus couldn't love others. Despite the past, it was wonderful to see the changes God had made in her life. That Sunday, the changes were obvious; I saw firsthand God's will being carried out. The person who was once cold and bitter was kind and loving.

Her contented look told me she was at peace with God and herself. She asked me to sit on her bed, and she told me that my dad had visited her the night before and that she was tired of fighting for her life every day. She said she was ready to join my dad in heaven.

I was sure that when my dad visited her, he had been relieved to find that the person he had fallen in love with years before had returned and that she had finally let go of what had held her in bondage to this world and was prepared to join him in heaven.

We spoke for hours, and it was the most inspiring and pleasant conversation we had ever had. I believe my mom could tell that I had forgiven her and that she had no reason to bring up forgiveness in our conversation. I had taken care of her in many ways during her time of sickness because I loved her. Besides, there was no reason for her to ask forgiveness; I had forgiven her years earlier. I didn't want unforgiveness to rob me of my peace and joy. Letting go all the negativity we bottle up inside gives us freedom to live our lives as we should.

She kissed me on the cheek and told me she loved me. She made me promise I would meet her in heaven when my life on earth was over. I was sad that I was losing my mom, but I rejoiced knowing that God looked beyond our faults and failures, forgave our sins, and granted our needs.

She needed healing, and God was healing her by taking her home. In heaven, we'll have new bodies free of pain and sickness. God always knows what is best for his children. She was scheduled for release the next day after a four-hour dialysis session and one other short procedure. I went to work knowing I would be off in time to pick her up.

But while I was at work, a woman called from the hospital with the sad news they had lost my mom during the procedure. I was sad but at the same time relieved that her suffering was over. I will always be grateful that God gave me the opportunity to see that all was well with her soul and that she was ready to make the journey toward heaven.

While making her funeral arrangements, I kept hearing a voice in my head telling me to look inside the family Bible, where Mom had kept important papers such as our birth certificates. Since all but one of my siblings had move out, I wondered what could have been in the Bible, but I've always listened to that little voice. I flipped through the family Bible and found a letter she had written to her children.

I was so glad God had been mindful of that because I had her letter read at her service. As we all sat together at her service, it was as if she were talking to all of us. If anyone had any doubts about our mom's salvation, this would put those feelings to rest.

A Message for My Children

I am writing this because I don't know when I will leave you. I just want my family to know that I have gone to live with Jesus, and all of you can come too if you live for him. The road is straight and narrow, and few will find it, but seek and you shall find. Ask Mr. Street to sing the song "Family Circle" at my funeral. Maybe it will bring some of our family closer to God.

I love you all with all my heart, but I was tired all the time just fighting for my life day after day, and I'm looking for a haven of rest. I hope we will all be together again in heaven someday. We will sit down by the river of life and rest a while.

I want all my family to be there. Just trust in God, and we will live again forever never more to be apart. I want all my children to love and help each other anyway they can. Always be kind to everyone you meet no matter who they are. Jesus will bless you for it.

Lift people up. Never put them down no matter what they have done. Help them if you can. The Bible is the key to the city that we cannot enter without God. Only through God's love and forgiveness do old things pass away and all things become new.

I love you all.
Mother

14
From the Mountaintop to the Valley

Life went on after my mom died. Our family was living in a two-bedroom mobile home. The more the boys grew, the more our mobile home seemed to shrink. One day, I started looking at house plans. I knew it was a dream that was more than likely out of our reach, but I looked anyway. I had witnessed God open all the doors necessary for me to open my salon, so I had no doubt that if it was God's will, the same would be true for a house.

I picked out my home plans and gave them to God. My mom had left us three acres of land, so we had a building site, but we didn't have a right-of-way to the property, so it was more of an island than a legitimate place to build.

But it wasn't long until we received a true prophecy from God. A Christian woman came up to my husband at work and prophesied to him that God had seen our faithfulness and would bless us. She told my husband that he shouldn't worry, that God was sending a man with a double chin to help us.

My husband shared that good news with us and said all we had to do was keep the faith. Though we had very little money, I stepped out on faith and begin looking for a lender for our house project. I always prayed that God would put stumbling blocks in my path if what I wanted wasn't his will for me. But as happened so many times before, over the weeks and months, I watched in amazement as God walked me through all the steps necessary to make my dream come true.

First, our neighbor gave us a deed to a right-of-way for our property, which then was no longer an island. Next, a lender qualified us for a loan. I had worked at the salon in town for only two years before opening my salon one year earlier. My husband and I didn't have a strong tax return to show our ability to repay the loan, but the lender trusted my honesty. He accepted our tax returns and a ledger of my day-to-day income over the past year that I had kept on index cards I used for writing down my customers' information.

Our biggest hurdle was yet to come. We needed $10,000 to begin construction—a huge obstacle. We found ourselves at an impasse; we couldn't borrow that much money and still qualify for our loan. I was so discouraged that I threw my house plans in the trash. I was only human, and that was a lot of money to come up with; it seemed impossible. We had only a week to give the lender our answer. I was ready to give up on my dream.

But just when things seemed impossible, God once again showed up right on time. I was at work and happened to see a car drive up. A man got out of his car and motioned for me to come outside. I should've known God had a plan in motion; apparently, he was testing my patience. Looking back, I wish I had done better with patience.

This was the man with the double chin God had prophesied to us about through the woman my husband worked with. He told me he felt my husband and I needed his help; he handed me a check for the amount we needed. He said we could pay him back at the end of construction. I was so happy that I wept and gave the man a big hug. I could hardly wait to go home and dig those plans out of the trash.

God knows our needs, and when we can't help ourselves, he uses others. We were able to save money during construction by my husband doing the plumbing and his brothers doing the heating, air, and electrical. At the end, we had enough left over from our loan to pay this wonderful, obedient man back in full.

God has blessed me in so many ways but not without letting me work hard along the way. To me, that was my blessing—being able to work hard. I was so happy for my family to finally have a home with room for our boys to grow up. I painted every wall, planted every flower, strategically placed every shrub, and made this house our home. Life was good. I had my health, a home, and my family. We were going to church regularly, serving God, and enjoying life. My husband and I were blessed with the ability to work every day. We worked to make our lives better, and it was all paying off. We wanted our sons to have a home they could be proud of. I was so happy to be able to provide running water, a place to take a bath, and a warm place to sleep. We even had carpet.

I don't think Satan can sit quietly by and watch good Christian families praise God and live contently. Satan targets the family because it is a symbol of strength and unity. But as long as families stick together with God in their hearts, Satan can pick at their foundations only from the outside.

And pick at our foundation is exactly what Satan did. We as Christians must be careful because Satan targets God's faithful children to destroy families. He don't appear in a red suit with a forked tail; he uses ordinary people to do his dirty work whether it be someone who is jealous of us and the blessings we have received or just people with lying tongues who set out to destroy us just because they can. I dealt with both.

We had enjoyed our home for only six years when I received the shock of my life. One night, my husband came home from working the night shift and woke me up to tell me it would be in my best interests to find our boys and myself a different place to live. He wanted a divorce. I was devastated. I felt I had been stabbed in the heart.

Later, he told me why he wanted a divorce. He said two women had told him I was having an affair. I was hurt even more when I found out that they were women I believed to be my friends. They had filled my husband's mind with a web of lies. I guess it was easy for him to believe these accusations because I worked so much. Owning your own business requires an exorbitant amount of time; it takes wearing many hats to keep everything running smoothly. At work, I was the maid and bookkeeper as well as my clients' stylist.

One of the women and her husband had gone out to dinner with my family on a few occasions. I kept asking myself why these women had told such lies. I had never been anything but a good friend to them. I saw firsthand the damage lies could do to a person's life. I asked God why Satan was having a field day destroying my life. Even people I had gone to church with for over twenty years were making false accusations about me.

When I questioned God about their actions and how anyone claiming to be a Christian would willfully try to hurt another, God replied to my spirit, "Some people with religious acts lack true salvation." I felt like every devil in hell was out to get me. All I had ever done was work every day to make my family's life better.

I had had the same opportunities as anyone else had to have affairs, but I never gave any of the opportunities a second thought. I would never trade my relationship with God or risk losing my family over an affair. Pleasures of the flesh are only temporary; your relationship with God and the love of your family are forever. I felt I was paying a price for something I wasn't guilty of. I prayed endlessly for God to give me the grace I needed to face each day.

Once again after coming so far, trying to build a life for my family, I felt that rocks on the mountain had given way and

I was sliding down to the valley. As I was sliding, God spoke to my heart: "People with lying tongues have set out to destroy you, but I will be at your right hand." That gave me the hope I needed, and I knew I would be okay. God was all I really needed.

My dad had always given me good advice. Once, he told me that God knows the truth no matter what others say, and God is the only one who matters. But I was angry, hurt, and bitter. Seeing my world shatter into a million pieces was devastating. I had worked endless hours to better the lives of my family, and to think I would lose it all was very hurtful. I found myself making a deal with God. I would deal graciously with losing everything and would forgive the two women who had started the landslide, but in return, all I asked was that I wouldn't lose my children. God promises that he won't put more on us than we're able to bear. I could live without my things but not without my children.

I kept my promise to God, and with forgiveness and understanding in my heart, I started looking for a place to live. My husband never interfered with the boys living with me, and though I was saddened by the family living apart, I never said an unkind word about him to our boys.

I had to stay in a specific school district so my teenagers wouldn't have to change schools. I had never considered living in town, but one day, I drove down a street near my salon on my way to lunch and saw a little two-bedroom house for sale in a perfect location. My sons could walk to my salon, and if they needed me, I would be close by.

I didn't know how I would be able to buy it since my name was already attached to a mortgage, but you'd think by then I would have at least guessed God had a plan. I met with the owner at the house. I knew it was the perfect home for us before I finished looking at it. It had been built in the early sixties, but I saw its potential. I love projects; after all, "Idle hands are evil hands," my daddy used to say. Besides, projects would be great therapy for me over the years to come. I told the owner about my situation, and he said he would be willing to owner finance until my other house sold. Amazingly, he offered me a payment that was well within my budget.

It amazes me that God always has a plan and puts the right people in our paths at just the right time like my sister showing up with the down payment. God had already taken care of everything I had worried about. My sister and I cleaned my new place for days. God knew that my making this house a home for my two boys and me would be great therapy.

We moved in. I was either working in the yard or painting walls in all my spare time. Our little house was all we needed, but it was hard leaving the home I had worked so hard to get. Starting over is hard to do all by yourself; I had to let go and let God continue to control my life. We had food and shelter, and that's all we really needed. Our wants and needs are different things. God promises to meet our needs, and he did just that. God even sent a pastor's wife to my salon with a scripture that I will forever hold dear to my heart. She was obedient, and God used her to let me know he was mindful of what I was going through. The scripture is Psalms 91; it reminds me that we serve an awesome God.

My boys were soon grown and left home for college to pursue their passions. My oldest boy went to flight school in Florida, and my youngest went to diving school in Seattle.

I have always known where my help came from, and I don't hesitate to ask for help. I know that when we ask God for something, the answer isn't always what we want to hear. That isn't comforting until we look back years later. If God would've given me everything I thought was good for my life, it would've been a disaster.

We don't know what tomorrow holds, but if we are children of God, we know who holds tomorrow. His promises are true, and they last forever.

The best part about serving God is that he loves us all the same; he will do for you what he will do for me. Sometimes, we face trials we don't understand. Sickness and hardship knock on our doors from time to time. Some of our trials are designed to make us stronger, but we can become weak carrying the load and wonder if God is listening to our prayers. During some of my hardest trials, I felt heaven was made of brass and my prayers were just bouncing off it. But going through such times helped me realize I needed an even closer walk with God. I read my Bible and talked to God more frequently during my trials. When you are on the mountaintop, life seems easy, but when you're in the valley, your faith is put to the test.

15
A Story of Miracles

Polycystic kidney disease runs in my family; my mom passed it along from her dad. Cysts grow and multiply until they shut down the kidneys. Little was known about the disease in the fifties, when my grandfather died of the disease; he never had the opportunity for treatment and passed away at an early age.

My mom was in her early fifties when she was diagnosed with it. It took numerous tests to finally pin down the actual disease. I fear that if my mom had known about this dreaded disease, she would've chosen not to have children. There is no known cure for the disease, but a kidney transplant is a viable alternative, and it can be treated with dialysis that filters your blood to purify it.

My mom also had a heart disease, and the treatment was extremely hard on her heart. She lived for only three years on dialysis before she passed away. One of my brothers was diagnosed with polycystic kidney disease in his early thirties, and it was a very difficult time for him. His life changed forever. I thank God for his beautiful wife he had met at a young age. She has been by his side all these years. They are Christians, but even with faith and understanding, this is a very hard trial for anyone to go through.

My brother and I would pray without ceasing. I would go to

the altar every week at church and lift him up to God. I loved him; he was my brother, and I shed many tears over his hardship and sickness. All I could do was pray, but I did so and believed in scripture for his healing. I had experienced my own healing, so I knew God could heal my brother; I just didn't know when. When things would get bad and it seemed all our hopes were lost, I would pray to God to let me be like the cedars of Lebanon. I wanted to be grounded in my faith so if my brother needed to lean on me, I could handle his weight.

His body was getting weaker, and so was his heart. I went to church one Sunday night with an overwhelming feeling that something good was coming from God. When it was time for the altar call, the Spirit of God told me to go pray for my brother. Something about that visit to the altar was different. The Spirit of God told me to tell my brother to read Ecclesiastes, in which God talked about a time and season.

As we were praying, one prayer warrior gave me a hug and said my brother's kidney was on its way. I said, "God, I claim this healing in Jesus's name."

I could hardly wait to get home from church to give my brother a call to share the good news. He was a little hesitant to believe me after being sick for so long. He had been on dialysis for over five years, but I thanked God for his message and with faith believed it would come to pass.

The next Saturday, my brother called with news—the Chapel Hill Medical Center had told him that a woman had passed away and that her kidney was a perfect match. He went in immediately for surgery, and on Valentine's Day, he got the perfect gift of love. The surgery went so well that he never even had to go into intensive care.

We serve an awesome God if we only put our trust in him. Faith unlocks the door to the many blessings God has for us. It has been over twenty years, and that kidney is still working.

We humans have trouble with patience and faith, but we need to remember God has perfect timing.

Another brother of mine went through a very difficult time when he got sick. It can be a very hard and depressing time when life changes drastically. He was a hard worker, but when he went on dialysis, he could no longer work. He was used to working every day and supporting his family. It wasn't long after he got sick that he lost his family and that his home went back to the bank. He had to find a less-expensive living arrangement. Though he lost his home and his land he had worked hard for, he remained positive; his faith never wavered. His love for God remained the same. I continued to pray daily for God to send him a transplant. After just over eight years, my prayers were answered.

One day, God spoke to my heart; he told me to read in Joel. I took my Bible out and started to read. I knew God was preparing my brother for a transplant. I was so humbled that God had shared that with me that I could hardly work; all I could do was cry. I knew I had to act on my faith and share this with him. I was scared and didn't want to give him false hope, but at the same time, I knew we served a God who could do all things.

He was the same God he had been twenty years earlier when he told me about my other brother's transplant. The scripture God gave me was perfect for him, so I had to call him with the good news. I told him that the scripture in Joel was for him and just to claim his healing. That's how faith works; we have to recognize and believe what God shows us.

A week later, I got the call I had been waiting for. My brother said, "You'll never guess where I am." He was so excited that he quickly said he was in Charlotte, North Carolina. I knew he was at the medical center. A young man had passed away in Asheville, North Carolina, the night before. My brother was a perfect match for his kidney, and that surgery would give him his life back. He went through surgery that day, and just like my other brother, he never had to go into intensive care. It has been years now, and all is well with him. God will work miracles in our lives, but we must have faith and believe.

I started having some health issues. I would occasionally have some bright-red blood show up in my urine. I felt fine, but with all the kidney problems in our family, I knew I shouldn't ignore the problem. Because my doctor knew my family history, he immediately thought I had polycystic kidney disease. I wanted to know the extent of my illness, so I asked to be referred to a specialist. I was prepared for whatever the answer might be. I went in for my appointment, and they injected dye in my veins and scanned me for cysts and tumors.

It was a long couple of weeks before I received my results. The urologist scheduled a cystoscope for the day I was to receive my results to confirm what had shown up during my testing. He told me I needed to be admitted to the hospital the next day to have a tumor on my bladder removed. In spite of that terrifying word *cancer,* God gave me peace.

The word *cancer* normally would have scared me to death especially after having watched my dad die from this horrible disease. The only way I can explain it is that when you have God in your heart, you know you're going to a better place when you die, a comforting feeling.

I had surgery the next day, and everything went well. I went home and followed the doctor's orders, but I knew I couldn't take more than two weeks off work. I thank God that he gave me the strength I needed to get back to work. Most of my customers never even knew I'd had surgery just two weeks earlier.

I put a smile on my face and powered through the day. I recited verses to myself that related to my situation. I was soon feeling much better and on the road to recovery. I have always relied on God to carry me through tough times. On the days I felt I couldn't put one foot in front of the other, I held onto the amazing strength and courage that can come only from our Father in heaven. I put the whole ordeal behind me, and soon, days turned into years. I consider the cancer just a bump in the road, possibly even a test of my faith.

When God heals you, it is forever. That was not the first time God had healed my body, and in all cases, the healing left no evidence of there ever having been a problem. My cancer was no exception. I return every year for a checkup, and from the very first cystoscopy, there has been no evidence of cancer—not even a scar due to my surgery. I praised God for perfectly healing my body. New doctors I go to say that if there weren't records of the surgery, they wouldn't believe I had had it.

I'll have my bladder checked every year, but I don't expect to find any problems. God is good. We'll all walk through trials, but if we have faith in God, we'll never walk through them alone. My symbol of hope is a butterfly. Every time I see one, I'm reminded that we serve a God who gives us a second chance.

16
Faith without Boundaries

As the years went by, I became discontent with life. The economy had taken a real downturn, and life was a struggle. God saw my discontent and started dealing with me about a change, something radical for a fresh start in life. But I had spent nearly fifty years in the same little town where I had grown up; I was in my comfort zone, and it was hard to think outside my little world.

But the economy had taken a huge turn for the worse. The majority of the workers in our town were involved in the furniture and textile industries, but their work had been sent to different countries leaving a lot of hard-working people without jobs. Few could afford a $10 haircut.

My children were busy with their own lives; my oldest was living and working in Tennessee, and the other was in Iraq. The decisions I had to make affected only me and my dog, Wendy, a Boston terrier. I prayed earnestly for months for God to give me answers. I never make decisions without praying and seeking God's favor. I had always told God that I wanted to be a willing vessel he could use in his ministry. For years, I had done just that in my salon, but I found myself with a rock in my shoe that I couldn't get out. I witnessed to people every day on my job.

God always sent me the best clients—99 percent Christians, so it made my job easy; we shared Jesus all day long.

Having been independent most of my life, it was natural for me to be very dependent on God. He is my courage, my source of strength. I have always depended on him to show me what he wants me to do with my life and to put stumbling blocks in my path if I was headed down the wrong path. My life would surely have been a disaster without his guidance. I always listen for that voice within for instruction and direction. Time and again as I was praying, that inner voice would simply say, "Go to Alaska, and I will restore your soul to the mountaintop." I just knew I wasn't hearing that voice correctly. With very little money and just a dog for moral support, I couldn't possibly move to Alaska. That would have meant stepping out of my comfort zone and having faith without boundaries.

But in some of my hardest times, God made himself so real to me that I had no doubt about him. If God was ready for a change in my life, I had to have faith and step out of my comfort zone.

Sometimes, God has a better plan for our lives because he knows our future and knows what's best for his children. We must trust him from one stepping stone to the next. God has always confirmed things to me through other people. I hadn't told anyone about my thoughts because I didn't want to worry anyone.

Just before my birthday my youngest son called me from Iraq. "Hey, Mom. You want to know what I'm getting you for your birthday"? I said, "No." He said, "You know how you've always wanted to go to Alaska? Well, I'm buying you a ticket." I was blown away. I hadn't had a vacation in twenty years. I had taken only two weeks off work after my cancer surgery. He told me he would even pay me a week's wages because he knew I couldn't afford to take a week off work.

All that seemed really affirming because God had already

spoke to my heart and told me to go to Alaska. So I knew God had a plan, and it was official—I was going to Alaska. I started making deals with God because the reality of actually making such a radical change in my life suddenly petrified me. I said, "Okay, God, I agree that I need a change, but what do you think about me staying a little closer to home? How about if I go to Charlotte, North Carolina?" Charlotte was only a one-hour drive from home, and it was where my son who worked in Iraq lived when he was home. I decided to apply for work at six salons there; I had twenty years' experience in the beauty industry, so I didn't think I'd have a problem being offered a job. I planned to go to Alaska in November and apply at six salons there. Whoever called me first was how I'd know if God really wanted me to go to Alaska.

I always had a desire to see Alaska, but how did it suddenly translate into living there? I now know God convinced me to go to Alaska when I did because Novembers there are cold and dark. I did a little research and determined I'd have snow up to my knees. I thought, *Land of the midnight sun my foot*. But God had provided everything I needed, so I would be obedient and go. I got on the plane in November 2009 not knowing what was in store for my life.

Not knowing anyone in Alaska took me way out of my comfort zone; it would just be God and me on this adventure. My faith was being tested beyond my comprehension. I went to Alaska not to vacation but on a leap of faith. I rented a car and applied for positions at five salons in Anchorage, Alaska's most populous city; more than 40 percent of the state's population lived there.

On March 27, 1964, a magnitude 9.2 earthquake hit Anchorage and killed 115 people. The earthquake lasted nearly five minutes. It isn't uncommon for people in Anchorage to experience earthquakes, but that's something I'd never dealt with back home.

Before going to the sixth salon, I stopped at a beauty supply to see what products were available and compare prices with those in North Carolina. I noticed a woman at the checkout line I felt I needed to talk to. It wasn't hard for me to spark a conversation because over the years, I had become quite a chatterbox. I asked her where she worked, and she said at a salon in the nearby town of Eagle River, about twenty miles northeast of Anchorage. I had a great feeling about it and could hardly wait to go there the next day.

The drive out to Eagle River was amazing; it looked like a winter wonderland because it had snowed during the night, but that made the drive hazardous especially for someone with absolutely no experience driving in snow. In the south, when any amount of snow fell, everything was closed and people just stayed home.

My small rental car didn't have studded tires. I thought, *Oh my! What have I gotten myself into?* I had only so much time in Alaska, so I pressed on. I felt compelled to complete my mission no matter what it took.

Talk about praying earnestly, I talked to God the whole twenty miles with white knuckles gripping the steering wheel. I was on a beautiful journey, but it seemed to take forever. I saw cars that had slid off the highway, and some were upside down.

By the time I got there, I was so shaken up that I didn't get a very good look at Eagle River. The salon was a small, family-owned operation, and I immediately felt this was where I was supposed to work. The owner told me there weren't any stations available for rent then, so I gave her my name and number and told her I was looking to start in January. I took her business card and told her to please notify me if something became available before the end of January. I put her card in my purse thinking of it more of a souvenir than an actual lead. I left there feeling proud of myself—I had done what I had set out to do.

The week went by fast, and I was soon back home. I knew

God had a plan for me, but I wasn't 100 percent convinced what it was; all I knew is that I had a rock in my shoe I couldn't shake. God gives us free will, and we make our choices with the opportunities he puts before us. I talk to God as if I'm talking to my best friend; he understands my strengths and weaknesses. He knows my serious thoughts and my witty self. After all, he created me. I let God know that I was acting in good faith by applying for my Alaska cosmetology license and had decided that whoever called first was where I'd go to work. Deep inside, I hoped God would open up a door for me in Charlotte so I could stay close to my comfort zone.

I got back into my daily routine and tucked that business card away in my workstation. I couldn't imagine leaving my coworker, a fine Christian woman I had worked beside for seventeen years, and our salon clients were like family. I told her about my plans, and we cried for days, but she was a Christian who totally understood.

I told her that if I found a job somewhere else, she should keep the salon because she was already established there. I continued to work for the next month not knowing what God had in store for me.

I have always wanted to do God's will for my life, to be a willing vessel, someone he could use for his glory. This was a huge task I felt I needed to undertake. Over the next month, I cried and prayed because giving up my life as I knew it to trust God with the next step was overwhelming. As I prayed to discover God's will, I was pointing out all the reasons I couldn't go. I had no money saved to float me while I built a clientele. Being self-employed is scary—no guarantee of income.

But I believed that God was faithful and that he'd never take me out on a limb and leave me hanging. I had to believe God was in charge, and I had to be obedient. He had surely proven himself over and over in my life, but because my parents were deceased and I feared failure, I really had to talk this over with

God. As I was praying, that inner voice spoke to my heart: "I am your heavenly Father, and I own everything." I knew I wasn't to fear whatever my next move would be.

Just over a month later, I received an Alaska cosmetology license. I thought that had gone rather smoothly. I was starting to feel as if no one would call about a job from either location. I felt I might just stay home in my little corner of the town where I had been raised.

The next day after receiving my cosmetology license, the phone rang; the salon owner in Eagle River said she had a station for rent. There it was again, the petrifying fear of actually doing something radical. Should I accept the challenge God laid out for me in Alaska? I did have free will in the matter, but I felt I had to follow the path God had set before me, so I planned on ending the year at my salon in North Carolina on December 31, 2009. I would be obedient and leave for Alaska in January 2010. I had served God since I was nine and had seen many things happen in my life, so I knew God had a perfect plan, but I was only human, and it's hard to have faith when you can't see the end. I suppose that's why it's called faith.

I started preparing for my move to Alaska. I found a woman in Anchorage who rented rooms; it would have been financially impossible for me to rent an apartment. Moving to Alaska was going to be the hardest thing I had ever done; it would be a true test of faith. Renting a booth from a salon in Alaska felt more like moving to a foreign country than another state.

Booth rental worked the same in Alaska as it did in North Carolina, but the rent in Alaska, $800 a month, was quite a bit more than I was use to in North Carolina. It would take a couple of years for me to get established in Alaska. I planned to keep my house in North Carolina as a backup plan; I wanted to hang onto it as long as I could. I was already turning my and my dog's lives upside down, and I felt hanging onto a little security wouldn't be admitting I didn't have faith in God's plan. After all,

God asks us to have the faith of only a mustard seed. I at least had that even with hanging onto my security blanket.

I had two weeks to prepare for my adventure. I wanted to end my tax season in North Carolina. That was the big portion of my motivation for not leaving until after the first of the year.

My coworker bought my salon for $5,000, so after a one-way ticket to Anchorage and paying someone to drive my car to Alaska, I had a grand total of $3,000 to start my new life with. It was the biggest leap of faith I had ever taken. With a little bit of courage and a whole lot of faith, I was going 5,000 miles outside my comfort zone. I hadn't researched the cost of living in Alaska; I knew it would be more than it was in the south, but I was operating on blind faith. I knew this was God's perfect plan, and I was obligated to allow God to use me as he saw fit.

In early January 2010, Wendy and I boarded a plane to start our adventure in the far north. This leap of faith would prove harder than I had ever imagined. I landed in Anchorage, and the woman from whom I had rented the room picked me up at the airport. Everything was so different than I was used to. I saw snow piled higher than cars everywhere I looked. It was dark and bitter cold; it was hard to adjust to so much darkness. My dog was in as much shock as I was.

When we were carrying my suitcases into the house, the woman said she had rented the room to some man who was moving to Alaska because of a job. I guess she hadn't taken me seriously though I had kept in touch with her as my plans came together. I had no choice but to reside in her cluttered garage with just enough room for a blowup mattress I bought and a kennel for Wendy. At least she didn't try to park her car in there.

I questioned my decision to move to Alaska, but I rented a car and went to work as soon as I was settled in. Wendy found a canoe propped up on sawhorses in the backyard. The canoe still had some grass underneath it, so at least she had some relief from all the snow.

Every morning, the blowup mattress I had purchased was flat, and Wendy and I were lying on the concrete floor. If you have ever lain on a concrete floor in a garage in the middle of winter in Alaska, you know what I mean when I say, "I can't imagine it being any colder on the ground outside." But I didn't have money to buy a bed, so that would have to do. It was tiring living out of a suitcase, and even harder was adjusting to the fact I had been allowed only two suitcases with my airline ticket, so my clothing was limited. It was hard to dress like a professional everyday living out of a box.

Despite the difficulties, I began to settle in and adjust to my new life. I was starting to wonder where my car was. I wasn't happy when I found out that the person I had paid to drive it up had gotten into an accident, so I had to continue to rent a car longer than I had planned.

My only outlet was my job, and I looked forward to it every day. The drive out to Eagle River was beautiful when it wasn't snowing and I wasn't swiveling my head around trying to avoid getting smashed into by cars that seemed to be sliding toward me from every direction. Working in Anchorage would have meant a shorter commute, but I felt strongly that God's plan for me was in Eagle River.

I knew I was supposed to work at that particular salon, but I feared signing a contract for a year at $800 a month. I began to feel overwhelmed. I prayed and prayed for God to show me what to do. I kept reminding myself that if I did my part, God would do his. I had given up my job in North Carolina to go on this journey of faith, so all I could do was move forward.

The owner of the salon had given me two weeks to get settled in before I was asked to sign the contract. On my way to work on the day I was to sign the contract, I talked to God about my situation. I have always asked God to show me a sign whenever I was faced with a tough decision. I asked God to send me one customer that day if this was where I was supposed to be. I was dreading signing the contract and planned to put it off all day hoping to get a sign from God. I was sitting at the front desk making other hairdressers' appointments when a woman walked in. I asked if I could help her, and she looked right at me and said, "You are supposed to cut my hair."

That took me by surprise. After she was in my chair, she shared that she was in the mission field, so that let me know she was a Christian. She gave me the answer I had been looking for. She said she was on her way to another salon when God spoke to her heart telling her to turn around and come to the salon I was at. God told her to tell the person sitting at the desk that she was supposed to cut her hair. This was a true sign from God that this was where I was supposed to be.

17
The Plan Starts Coming Together

I signed the contract that would keep me in Alaska for the year. I had to work seven days a week at the salon to build my clientele one person at a time. The woman who owned the house I was living in made custom jewelry that she sold in shops throughout Alaska. I also had experience making jewelry; I had made and sold jewelry at my salon in the south to supplement my income. I helped her with her jewelry and in return got a break on my rent. That proved to be a blessing and a curse.

I made jewelry until 1:00 in the morning and worked every day at the salon. The more exhausted I became, the harder it was not to question my decision to come to Alaska. I read God's Word every night by flashlight looking for answers. At one point, I said, "God, I know I must have misunderstood you. This can't possibly be what you would have me do. I want to be obedient, and you said go and I will restore you, but this is ridiculous. I still have my home and comfortable bed in North Carolina. Sleeping on the floor and working seven days a week is beginning to wear on me."

My only entertainment was taking my dog through the drive-thru at a fast-food restaurant on Saturday night; she was my Saturday night date. The first year was the toughest, but I managed to build a customer base one customer at a time. I had to stay positive, work hard, and keep the faith that whatever God's plan was for my life would soon come into focus.

In my first year, I managed to save enough money to bring my two sons to Alaska for a vacation. We had never taken a vacation as a family, so that was a wonderful treat for us. I had stayed up late every night making jewelry, and it had given me an opportunity to get to know the woman I was renting my room from. As it turned out, she was a great woman, and we became good friends. She was very Alaskan. She had trophies of bear, sheep, and caribou from her hunts across Alaska hanging on her walls. She was also an avid angler and would take trips to the Kenai Peninsula every summer to stock up on salmon for the winter.

The Kenai Peninsula juts out from the coast of south-central Alaska and extends approximately 150 miles south from Anchorage. I made arrangements to tag along on one of her trips and took my two sons along. We had a wonderful time. We fished the infamous Kenai River, the longest river on the peninsula. It runs eighty-two miles westward from Kenai Lake in the Kenai Mountains and through the Kenai National Wildlife Refuge and Skilak Lake to its outlet into the Cook Inlet. The Kenai River is the most popular sports fishing destination in Alaska. This country was all new to me, so actually, we could have been anywhere.

We were after red salmon, the premier salmon for eating, canning, and smoking. Catching your limit of these fish helps provide food for your family. My boys and I were greenhorns at fishing the Alaskan waters, and it was best for us not to go during the day. That was when fishing the Kenai was considered combat fishing—fisherman stood arms' lengths from each other trying to catch this elusive salmon.

It was great having my sons enjoying this great adventure

with me. While we were waiting until midnight to go fishing to avoid the crowds, we drove to nearby Skilak Lake and enjoyed beautiful scenery and a campfire. We ate roasted hot dogs and marshmallows until we were stuffed.

It gets dark only briefly in the summer in Alaska, so the days are long and somewhat exhausting. As soon as midnight came, the woman felt safe taking us to the river to try our hand at fishing. That was important to her, but it meant something different for us; we were enjoying quiet time together. Our lives had taken us in different directions, and for us just to be together was amazing. My sons had traveled from Tennessee and North Carolina to the Kenai River, so they were exhausted. I decided we should all lie on the river bank and look up at the beautiful Alaska night sky God had blessed us with. With my sons laying their heads on my arms, I felt so special that night. My heart was full of gratitude for the two blessings God had miraculously given me.

We were even able to take a halibut fishing charter out of Homer, a city on the peninsula 218 miles southwest of Anchorage. It was known as the halibut fishing capital of the world, and it was nicknamed "The End of the Road," an appropriate nickname because it was literally as far as you could drive southwest from Anchorage.

I wanted my sons to see all the beauty they could during their short visit to Alaska. We had some fabulous fishing at Homer Spit, which was surrounded by ocean. We went a long way out on the ocean. We saw lots of wildlife and caught some of the largest fish we had ever seen. Our fishing guide, who was very knowledgeable and energetic, helped us stay focused on what we were doing, and no one got sick. I wanted my boys to enjoy their stay in Alaska. I had an ulterior motive; I hoped they would want to live there someday. My plan was working—they both liked Alaska, and my oldest son saw an opportunity to advance his flying career there and decided to stay.

Thank God I was starting to get established because I found myself needing an apartment big enough for the two of us. I knew it wouldn't be that hard for him to find a job because he could fly helicopters and fixed-wing aircraft. I was so happy not to be alone anymore; having a family member there gave me the optimism I had been missing.

I found an apartment in Eagle River; I could finally quit driving twenty miles each way in dangerous conditions. I had even saved up enough money to buy mattresses from the Salvation Army store. I furnished my apartment one piece at a time, and it soon started to resemble a home.

God's plan still wasn't exactly clear, but I was finding it easier to wait for it to present itself. I wasn't sure when the restoration portion of God's plan would emerge, but I was gaining faith that he did in fact have a plan. I missed my family in the south; I was used to having a support system. If I needed someone, he or she was always nearby. I was still holding onto my home in the Carolinas for no other reason than I wanted a safety net, but I felt guilty about that; I felt I was failing my faith by keeping a backup plan. However, my past hadn't exactly given me the confidence to get out on a limb without a safety rope.

18
All in God's Time

During the time I spent alone with God and Wendy, I went back to the potter's wheel to get all my rough edges of life smoothed off. I'd struggled for so many years that I had lost hope and faith in everything except God. I just kept saying, "God, I know you have a plan for my life. Reveal it and your servant will obey."

One beautiful summer day, I was sitting outside the salon enjoying the sun when a gentleman walked in. It was my turn for a walk-in, so I went inside. The man went up to the desk, and before he had a chance to say anything, the woman who owned the salon told him she didn't need whatever he was selling. His face fell. He just stood there. He slowly started to turn and walk away. I approached him and asked, "May I help you?" He said, "I'd like to get my hair cut because I need to get on an airplane and see my mother."

I said, "Come with me back yonder. My station's in the back." My workstation there was a perfect spot for me since I was always sharing Jesus with anyone who sat in my chair. I always shared the great things God had done for me. Sometimes, a word of encouragement is just as good as a great haircut. It makes my life worthwhile to see my customers with happy smiles and glad hearts. I didn't treat this guy different from the way I treated any other customer. I was pretty good at reading people by then, and one look into his deep-blue eyes told me he had a broken heart and spirit. I'm pretty easy to talk to, and it didn't take him long to tell me that his dad had passed away that morning and that he had lost his sister just a few months earlier to cancer.

It was perfect timing for me to share how God had carried me through the grief of losing my parents and how only God could give us the grace we need during our times of grief. God has blessed me with a great love and compassion for people, so I always trusted him to give me just the right words to say to people in my chair. I may look at them as strangers at first, but we are all God's children who need each other, and it's amazing how a word of kindness or a simple hug can make such a difference in someone's life.

When I finished his haircut, I gave him a hug just as I had done for many customers over the years. I told him that I would be praying for him as he walked through the death of his father and that God would give him the same grace he gave me. After I checked him out at the front desk, I went to the back of the salon and started seeking God on this guy's behalf. I had never met him before, but I knew he needed the strength that came only from God.

In my career, I hear so many stories both happy and sad said about people's lives. When God chose this career for me, he also gave me a great love for people and the ability to read their spirits by looking into their eyes. That lets me know what kind of person I'm dealing with. He also gave me the boldness that has come in very handy in my line of work. This job is far more than just doing people's hair. If one of my clients has a health problem or any other issue, I pray with them or for them; that's something God built into my service that I share with anyone in my chair.

I have seen God do some great things over the years. I follow up on the trials in people's lives; the next time I see them,

I expect to hear good news. Though my faith is sometimes as small as a mustard seed, I believe we'll get good results in God's timing. I didn't know if I would ever see that man again, but I had faith that God would help him through this dark time in his life.

A few weeks later, the salon owner told me that the man had emailed the salon. She said he wanted her to tell me thanks for being such a pillar of strength in the passing of his dad. He said he was a very shy person who kept his emotions to himself for the most part, but on the flight down to see his mother, he had opened up to the person next to him, and before he knew it, he was in a conversation with several rows of passengers. They all had something they wanted to share with him about their experiences with losses in their lives. He said that instead of the flight being full of pain and disappointment, it had been one of healing and love for others.

My phone didn't have email or text, so the only way the man could thank me for my prayers and words of encouragement was through the salon. I was so thankful that God had shown up on his behalf. My message back to him was simple; I said I was glad he and I shared the same friend.

He had told me on his first visit to the salon that he hadn't been to very many hair salons before; he had always gone to barbershops, but because of his emergency situation, he had stopped in at the first place he thought he could get a haircut. He said why he had wanted a haircut then; he was a second-generation bush pilot, and the company he worked for offered jump-seat privileges, but he had to follow the dress code. He wasn't used to dressing up; he'd worn work clothes his whole life.

What I didn't know was that the salon owner was trying to play matchmaker behind my back. Since I had no means of conversing with him, she was communicating with him on my behalf. She told him that I had been an inspiration for the salon and that he should get together for coffee with me sometime. I was mad at her at first for going behind my back and trying to arrange for me to meet someone I had seen only briefly, but she gave me an old phone of hers as part of her matchmaking plan. I'd never had the technology to send and receive emails from a phone until then.

I decided that if he came back for another haircut, I would give him my email address, and that all happened. I realize now that if I hadn't been working at that particular salon in Eagle River, I would have never met this gentleman. He was from Alaska, and I was from North Carolina, and neither of us was really comfortable in the new age of communication. I will always feel God had a plan for us to meet each other. It's sad and joyous at the same time to think God had used his father's passing for us to meet. We both believed there was only one God, one Jesus, and one Holy Spirit.

I wasn't looking for anyone to share my life with, but I couldn't have asked for a better person. Wendy bit him on the nose the first time he came to my apartment for dinner, but the way he handled that incident made me feel there was hope for our future.

A couple of years later, we married, and God has truly blessed us. I no longer had to wonder how God would restore me from all the brokenness I had gone through. I figure Satan had a real good time thinking that he would destroy me and that I would give up. What Satan didn't know was that I would tighten my boot straps and keep on walking my journey of faith.

My love for God is stronger than anything of this world. My relationship with him means more to me than houses or land. If you have ever been saved, Satan can still tempt you and try to get you to turn your back on God, but he cannot cross the blood line of Jesus Christ.

God told me he would restore me, and though at times I questioned him, I managed to hold onto the faith that he would do as he promised. When God told me to give up everything in the south and move to Alaska, that definitely tested my faith. I have since given up my safety blanket and sold my house in the south. Nothing worth doing is easy, but the trials I have endured have been worth every leap of faith.

A year after we were married, God opened a door for me to open a salon again, something I'd never dreamed would ever happen. I'm grateful that God opened every door and moved every obstacle to allow me to build a pulpit and continue spreading the Word of God. He gave me back everything I had sacrificed. I have a home in Alaska as well as my new salon.

God don't want us to be afraid to start over; it gives us a chance to build something better. I have been blessed with another great clientele and coworkers. I have kept my southern charm and added some country music. I am so proud of my salon, which has won various awards and recognitions, but what I'm mostly proud of is that the majority of the people who come through the door feel there's something comfortable about my salon. I know I am where God wants me to be at this time in my life because he has truly blessed my efforts.

When my youngest son decided to move to Alaska, I had everything I had in the south. Actually, I had more because my new husband has a son who is also a successful bush pilot, and I have grown to love him like my own sons. He also came with a bonus, a precious granddaughter I love very much.

I am also grateful that my youngest son had an opportunity to use his commercial diving skills diving for gold in the frigid waters off the coast of Nome. It was an adventure that let him try something new and exciting. He searched for gold in Nome for two summers, but the reward wasn't enough to justify it as a career. With money coming in sporadically and not being able to afford health insurance, he was in a very vulnerable position.

When you arrive at a small community no matter where it is, you are understandably looked upon as an outsider, and if you're there to harvest a natural resource and don't have any plans to move to that community, it's hard to fit in. My son was walking home from work one night and was attacked by some individuals who were fueled by alcohol and jealousy. They wanted to make it very clear he wasn't welcome to dive for their gold, and as a result, his leg was broken.

It is one of my daily prayers that God put a hedge of protection around my family. When I got the call about the attack, I was hurt and angry. I had raised my children to show love and respect for everyone. My boys have never been in any kind of trouble, and they show love and respect to whomever they meet. They inherited the personality God gave me when I started my career in the beauty industry. I've never met a stranger, and neither have they. It's hard for parents to see their children dealing with the world's harsh realities. It's hard enough to teach them to have love and respect for others when they aren't shown love and respect in return. I arranged for him to fly to Anchorage, where he could see a surgeon.

Since he didn't have any insurance and my husband and I didn't have a nest egg big enough to pay for his surgery, I was worried about the bill. All I could do was remember what the Bible says about the Lord—he is greater than any giant we face.

My only concern was to get my son's leg fixed. We found a doctor and made arrangements for a monthly payment plan. We didn't know any doctors in Alaska, so we just accepted the one my son was assigned.

The doctor did a great job, and my son was on his way to a full recovery. As a family, we prepared to make monthly payments to make sure the debt was paid. But when we opened our first bill from the medical office that had done the surgery, it was as though my life flashed back to opening the bill for my mom's surgery. We just broke down and started to cry; the bill showed a zero balance. The same God who had intervened for my mom had done the same for my son.

I couldn't be happier that God is in control of my life. If we all would learn to be obedient to God's call, we might find that the blessings we receive are bigger than we can imagine. God has always been true to his word in my life. Though my walk has not always being easy and I have been through many trials, I wouldn't trade anything for my journey with Christ.

What I want to share with everyone is that we must hold on tight to our faith throughout all our trials. We must look at our scars we have accumulated whether emotional or physical as reminders of victories we have won. We serve a God who will deliver us from our pain and suffering to victory.

About the Author

The author was born in humble surroundings in a small community in North Carolina. Armed with little more than her determined personality and her love for Jesus, she embarked on a lifelong journey to spread God's love. After becoming a cosmetologist, she began using her workstation as her pulpit to share Jesus with all who sat in her chair.